John W. Gray

Richard G. Rea

Auburn University

PARLIAMENTARY PROCEDURE:

a programed introduction

L. C. Catalog Card #63-17122

SCOTT, FORESMAN AND COMPANY Chicago, Atlanta, Dallas, Palo Alto, Fair Lawn, N.J.

PREFACE

Over 2000 years ago Socrates laid the foundation for programed learning in his method of teaching through dialog. Later, the great Roman teacher Quintilian defined the educational process as a "series of arranged victories." Sidney L. Pressey dusted off this idea and pointed the way toward what is today called "programed learning."

In these days of jammed classrooms and intellectually demanding curricula, it has become essential to use improved methods of instruction. Programed learning via a programed text is one such method. The programed text leads the student to understanding by a series of very small steps. It allows him to proceed at his own pace and provides him with immediate reinforcement of correct responses. Proceeding through the sequence of small steps, the student knows the required responses; he does not have to guess. Checking immediately against the printed responses, he is rewarded, achieving the "victories" of which Quintilian spoke, and his knowledge is reinforced.

This programed text attempts to present the essentials of parliamentary procedure in such a way that the student is able to gain a basic understanding. Frequent reference is made to *Robert's Rules of Order Revised*, where detailed information is provided. It is hoped that the material programed in this text will enable a student of parliamentary procedure to become a better member of an organization, to conduct meetings proficiently, and to make efficient use of *Robert's Rules of Order Revised*.

This text is divided into seven sets of frames. Set A, Introduction, presents a synoptic view of the origin and use of parliamentary procedure. Set B deals exclusively with the problems of conducting a meeting and the steps in the order of business. Sets C and D are devoted to the methods of making and amending a motion, with emphasis on the method of gaining the floor and voting procedures. Set E classifies each commonly used motion, giving its usage and its precedence in relation to the other motions. Set F discusses the essential officers of an organization and the qualifications and responsibilities for each office and offers a procedure for elections. Finally, Set G describes how to draw up a constitution and by-laws in organizing a club.

The authors are convinced that parliamentary procedure cannot be learned from a text only. The student must have an opportunity to apply the procedures in practice and under supervision. Through the student's use of PARLIAMENTARY PROCEDURE: A PROGRAMED INTRODUCTION as a self-instructional device, valuable classroom time can be saved for just such supervised practice.

This programed text has been tested at Auburn University and Louisiana State University, and thanks are extended to the speech departments of these universities. The authors are grateful for the assistance of a grant-in-aid from Auburn University to carry out the research, testing, and development of this text. Finally, we express our gratitude to the many students for their evaluation and testing of the program; to Mrs. Susan G. Rea for expert typing and proofreading of the manuscript; and to our wives for their constant faith and enthusiasm.

J.W.G.
R.G.R.

PRE-TEST ON PARLIAMENTARY PROCEDURE

The student can measure his progress by taking this test before starting the program and then retaking this test, reprinted on pages 109 through 111, after he has completed the program.

1. Where does the term "parliamentary procedure" come from?

2. List the steps in the order of business.

3. What is the procedure for gaining the floor in a meeting?

4. List the three ways in which a motion may be amended.

5. What is an amendment to the main motion called? What is an amendment to the amendment called?

6. What is a simple majority vote?

7. What is the simplest way to determine a two-thirds majority?

8. Number the following motions in their order of precedence.
   ____Amend
   ____Lay on the table
   ____Adjourn
   ____Previous question
   ____Recess
   ____Main motion proposing some new action
   ____Limit debate
   ____Question of privilege
   ____Fix the time of the next meeting
   ____Committee of the whole

9. What motion would you use to:
   a. Find out the proper procedure to make a motion.

b. Defend yourself against a personal attack.

c. Correct an error in procedure.

d. Override a ruling by the chair.

e. Gain information concerning pending business.

f. Nullify a motion passed at a previous meeting.

g. Dispose of another member's motion without voting on it after debate has begun.

h. Test the voting strength without actually voting on the relevant question.

i. Check the results of a voice vote.

j. Change your vote from "yes" to "no" on a motion just passed.

10. Write *P* for privileged motions, *S* for subsidiary motions, *M* for main motions, and *I* for incidental motions.

_____Previous question
_____Orders of the day
_____Limit debate
_____Object to consideration
_____Postpone indefinitely
_____Lay on the table
_____Take from the table
_____Suspend the rules
_____Postpone definitely
_____Withdraw a motion
_____Refer to a committee
_____Special order of business

11. What special qualifications must be met by a person moving to reconsider?

12. Name the two types of committees and explain how they differ.

13. Mark *T* for true and *F* for false.

_____Parliamentary procedure must be exactly the same for all organizations.

_____It is possible to change or rephrase another member's motion without amending it.

_____The chairman can take an active part in the meeting and voice his views at any time.

_____A motion that is laid on the table will automatically be brought up and voted on at the next meeting.

_____If the chairman is not sure what ruling to make, the safest thing for him to do is to call for a vote.

14. When can the chairman vote?

15. What book is the best reference manual on parliamentary procedure?

16. What is the final and supreme authority governing an organization?

17. List the articles commonly found in a combined constitution and by-laws.

CONTENTS

INSTRUCTIONS

This programed text is designed to teach basic parliamentary procedure by having you proceed step by step through the various phases. You are to begin with Set A, Introduction, and proceed, frame by frame, through the entire program. If you skip frames or fail to read each frame carefully, you may find yourself confused or unable to complete later frames. Follow these simple rules.

1. Read each frame carefully.

2. Note the underlined words and phrases. They are aids in completing many of the frames.

3. The number of blanks in the frame indicates the number of missing words. *Write* the missing word or words *in the space at the right*. Do not fill in the blanks in the frame.

4. The correct response to each frame appears at the end of the following frame. After writing in the response, check your answer. If you find yourself looking at the correct response *before* you have thought out and written down your answer, use a piece of paper to cover the frame below the one you are working on.

5. If you fail to complete a frame correctly, try to determine the reason for your error before proceeding to the next frame.

6. Work as much of the program as possible in one sitting.

7. If questions arise concerning the subject, refer to *Robert's Rules of Order Revised.*

To be sure you understand the procedure just outlined, here is an example:

1. The correct response to each frame appears at the end of the following ――――.   [write here]

―――――――――――――――――――――――――――――

2. After writing in the response in the space at the right, check your ――――.
frame

After reading frame 1, you should write the missing word in the space at the right (NOT in the blank after *following*) and then check your answer against the correct response printed at the end of frame 2. Only then should you proceed to frame 2.

INTRODUCTION

A1. Our democracy is based on government by public opinion, which is guaranteed expression by our freedom of speech. The privilege of expressing ourselves in public and in private on any issue is called our ⎽⎽⎽ ⎽⎽⎽ ⎽⎽⎽.

A2. In addition to this freedom of speech, we also have a responsibility to our fellow citizen not to hinder him in exercising the same ⎽⎽⎽ ⎽⎽⎽ ⎽⎽⎽.

freedom of speech

A3. We usually exercise this freedom of speech in public gatherings (club meetings, conventions, etc.) where we have the opportunity to *speak* as well as to ⎽⎽⎽ to what the other people have to say.
freedom of speech

A4. The best system of rules yet devised for conducting business within a group is called parliamentary procedure. These rules provide an opportunity to exercise freedom of ⎽⎽⎽.
listen

A5. The term "parliamentary procedure" comes from the British governing body called the ⎽⎽⎽.
speech

A6. The British Parliament developed a set of rules to keep order in their meetings. This set of rules was called ⎽⎽⎽ ⎽⎽⎽.
Parliament

A7. When the colonies were organized in America, they also needed rules for governing their meetings. They devised their own rules but still called these rules ⎽⎽⎽ ⎽⎽⎽.
parliamentary procedure

A8. The term "parliamentary procedure" comes from the ⎽⎽⎽ Parliament.
parliamentary procedure

A9. Parliamentary procedure guarantees that each individual has an opportunity to speak. When the time comes to stand up and be counted, _____ procedure provides the opportunity.
British

A10. The best system man has discovered for keeping order and giving each person the chance to be heard in business meetings is called _____ _____.

parliamentary

A11. Order can be maintained in a meeting by using parliamentary procedure. If a group, of any size, meets and debates a problem and the debate becomes unruly, then parliamentary _____ can be used to maintain order.
parliamentary procedure

A12. If a group consists of only a few members, it is less likely that parliamentary _____ will be needed to maintain order.
procedure

A13. The nature and purpose of a group's meeting will aid in determining whether or not _____ procedure should be used.
procedure

A14. If a group is trying to arrive at an answer acceptable to all of its members, then *group discussion* should be employed. Through _____ _____, consensus (agreement by all) can be attained.
parliamentary

A15. If the purpose of the group is to arrive at a solution in a very short time, then _____ procedure can be used to determine the will of the majority of the members.
group discussion

A16. If a group has unlimited time to decide on a solution and it is desirable for all members to participate in making the decision, then _____ discussion should be used in order to gain consensus.
parliamentary

A17. Parliamentary procedure protects the *minority* group in a meeting by giving those members an equal chance to voice their opinions. Therefore, parliamentary procedure not only determines the will of the majority but also protects the rights of the _____.

group

A18. Within a group using _____ procedure, each member's vote counts the same.

minority

A19. A member's *vote* counts as much as an officer's _____ when parliamentary procedure is used.

parliamentary

A20. Parliamentary procedure guarantees that each member will have an equal right to voice his opinion on a subject and an equal _____ in determining what the organization will do about each subject discussed.

vote

A21. Parliamentary procedure provides for free discussion of all subjects but limits the discussion to one *subject* at a time. One subject must be disposed of before another _____ can be introduced.

vote

A22. One of the best ways to maintain order in a business meeting is to use the rules provided in the system called _____ _____.

subject

A23. Parliamentary procedure might be compared with our traffic laws. The traffic laws tell us when to *stop*, and parliamentary procedure tells us when to be *silent*. The traffic laws tell us when to *go*, and parliamentary procedure tells us when to _____.

parliamentary procedure

A24. Without parliamentary procedure, we often find ourselves running into one another — speaking at the same time. Parliamentary procedure will help direct our traffic and prevent our speaking at the same _____.
speak or talk

A25. Traffic laws are designed to serve a certain group of people. In the same way, parliamentary procedure must be molded to fit the needs of the members of the _____ using it.
time

A26. It should be kept in mind that laws (rules) are for men and not _____ for laws.
group, organization, club, etc.

A27. Parliamentary procedure will never be the same for all *organizations*. If the members use parliamentary procedure, then it must be molded to fit the needs of the _____.
men

A28. The United States Steel Corporation would not use the same procedure in its meetings as would the local Lions Club. Parliamentary procedure will never be the same for all _____.
organization

A29. The idea is to make parliamentary procedure work for the organization and its members. It is necessary for each member to understand the basic rules involved so that he may participate in his organization's business _____.
organizations

A30. Many times individuals fail to participate in the discussion at a meeting because they do not know the *procedure* being used. Each person will be a more productive member if he learns the _____ and joins in the discussion.
meetings

A31. With a knowledge of the basic rules of _____ _____, an individual can freely participate in business meetings and feel as if he is receiving the full advantage of his freedom of _____.
procedure

A32. Each *citizen* in our democracy should exercise his freedom of speech, but he must exercise it responsibly. Our organizations, like our democracy, must be composed of responsible ____.

parliamentary procedure · speech

You are now ready to begin Set B, Conducting a Meeting. The answer to the last frame in Set A is given below.

citizens

Set B
CONDUCTING A MEETING

B1. To avoid *confusion* in business meetings, the members normally follow a definite order of business which is composed of eight steps to be followed from the beginning to the end of the meeting. By using these steps, _____ can be avoided in meetings.

B2. The order of business could be compared with the instructions of a do-it-yourself kit in which the different *steps* are numbered in sequence. The order of business is composed of eight _____ to be followed during the meeting.
confusion

B3. The order of business is composed of _____ steps.
steps

B4. This pattern of eight steps is called the _____ of _____.
eight

B5. The meeting must begin with step number _____ and end with step number _____.
order · business

B6. In molding parliamentary procedure to best serve the needs of a _____, it may be necessary to change the order and/or the number of steps in the order of business.
one · eight

B7. The first step in the order of business is the *call to order*. At the appointed time for the meeting to start, the chairman will _____ the meeting to _____.
group

B8. The chairman calls the meeting to order by saying, "The meeting will please come to order." This is the _____ step in the order of business.
call · order

B9. If the club meets on Thursday at 7:00 p.m., then at that time the chairman will _____ the meeting _____ _____.
first

B10. The order of business has _____ steps, and the first one is the _____ _____ _____.
call · to order

B11. The second step in the order of business is the *reading and approval of the minutes.* Some organizations have an invocation and roll call after the call to order and before the reading of the _____, but this practice is optional and is not considered one of the eight steps in the order of business.
eight · call to order

B12. If an organization wishes to begin its meetings with an invocation, the invocation should be included after the call to order but before the _____ and approval of the minutes.
minutes

B13. The roll call is necessary to determine if a *quorum* is present. A _____ is determined by calling the roll of the members to see if enough members are present to carry out the business of the organization. The _____ call is optional for each organization.
reading

B14. The quorum of an organization is the number of members that must be present in order to carry out the _____ of the organization.
quorum · roll

B15. Not all organizations have a roster of members; if an organization does not have a roster, then no _____ _____ could be taken.
business

B16. When a roll call is taken to determine whether or not a quorum is present, the quorum is based upon the *number* present at a meeting and not the _____ voting.
roll call

B17. If a quorum is necessary in order to conduct business, a ____ ____ is taken to determine the number of members present.
number

B18. The second step in the order of business is the *reading and approval of the minutes*. The chairman will say, "The secretary will please read the ____ of the last meeting."
roll call

B19. At the time the meeting is to start, the chairman will call the meeting to ____ and then have the secretary read the ____ of the last meeting.
minutes

B20. The minutes of the last meeting are a record of what business took place at the previous meeting. The reading and approval of the minutes is the ____ step in the order of business.
order · minutes

B21. The purpose of having the minutes read and approved is to recall to the members what was accomplished at the last ____.
second

B22. If the members agree that the minutes read are a true account of the last meeting, then the minutes are *approved*. The secretary will write the word "____" at the end of the minutes along with the date and his signature.
meeting

B23. If a member finds fault with the minutes, he may correct them by addressing the chair and stating his objections. After the corrections have been made, the secretary writes "____" at the end of the minutes along with the date and his

____.

approved

B24. Once the minutes have been read and approved by the organization, they become a permanent record of all business discussed and all action taken by the ____.
approved · signature

B25. The third step in the order of business consists of the *reports of standing committees,* which are the permanent committees of the organization. After the reading and approval of the minutes, the next step in the order of business is the ____ ____ ____ ____.
organization

B26. The standing committees are the ____ committees of an organization.
reports of standing committees

B27. Examples of standing committees could be: the finance committee, the membership committee, the public relations committee, etc. The reports from these committees constitute the ____ step in the order of business.
permanent

B28. The reports from the standing committees generally are read by the chairmen of these committees. The *order* in which the reports are given is dictated by the ____ in which the standing committees appear in the constitution.
third

B29. The fourth step in the order of business consists of the *reports of special committees.* The *special* committees are only temporary committees which are set up to investigate ____ problems of the organization.
order

B30. Examples of special committees could be: Valentine Banquet Committee, Junior Prom Decorations Committee, Ladies' Night Committee, etc. Reports from these committees constitute the ____ step of the order of business.
special

B31. The fourth step in the order of business consists of the ____ ____ ____ ____.
fourth

B32. These special committees are not *permanent* committees but ____ committees.
reports of special committees

B33. So far we have studied four of the eight steps in the order of business. Fill in the missing steps:
1. call to order
2.
3. reports of standing committees
4.

temporary

B34. Fill in the missing steps in the order of business:
1.
2. reading and approval of the minutes
3.
4. reports of special committees

2) reading and approval of the minutes 4) reports of special committees

---

B35. List the first *four* steps in the order of business.

1) call to order 3) reports of standing committees

B36. The fifth step in the order of business is *unfinished business*. By "unfinished business" we mean any business left over from a previous _____.

1) call to order 2) reading and approval of the minutes 3) reports of standing committees 4) reports of special committees

---

B37. If the business was not finished at the last meeting, it must be brought before the group again. This unsettled business is known as _____ _____.

meeting

B38. Bringing unfinished business up before the organization is the _____ step in the order of business.

unfinished (or old) business

B39. It is the duty of the chairman to see that all unfinished business is presented to the organization at the next _____.

fifth

B40. The sixth step in the order of business is *new business*. If a member wishes to propose something new, he must do it under the sixth step which is _____ _____.
meeting

B41. New business consists of anything that has not been brought before the club at a previous meeting. If a member wants to propose that the clubroom be painted and this idea has not been mentioned before, he will bring it up under _____ _____.
new business

B42. Under the heading of new business, as anywhere else in the order of business, only one subject (motion) can be considered at a time. If a member wishes to propose new business to the club, he will do it under step number _____ of the order of business.
new business

B43. Because of the large amount of fresh and recent information available to progressive organizations, more motions will probably be made under the step called _____ _____ than under any other step in the order of business.
six

B44. The seventh step in the order of business is *announcements*. When all of the new motions have been disposed of under step number six, then the floor is open for any member to make an _____.
new business

B45. The chairman may receive announcements before the meeting. He will then present these under step number _____ of the order of business.
announcement

B46. If a member wants to inform the organization of an item of interest to them, he will make this statement under step number seven of the order of business which is _____.
seven

B47. The eighth and last step in the order of business is *adjournment*. When the business has been completed, there must be a step provided to close the meeting. This step is called _____.
announcements

B48. When we adjourn, we close the _____.
adjournment

B49. Many clubs have a fixed time for ending their meetings. If this fixed time is 9:00 p.m., then the club must _____ its meeting at 9:00 p.m.
meeting

B50. The eighth step in the order of business is _____.
adjourn or close

B51. We have seen how the order of business is organized into _____ steps. These steps are followed in order to avoid _____ in the meeting.
adjournment

B52. Fill in the missing steps in the order of business:
1. call to order
2.
3. reports of standing committees
4.
5. unfinished business
6. new business
7. announcements
8. adjournment
eight · confusion, disorder, etc.

B53. Fill in the missing steps:
1.
2. reading and approval of the minutes
3.
4. reports of special committees
5. unfinished business
6.
7. announcements
8. adjournment
2) reading and approval of the minutes 4) reports of special committees

14

B54. Once again fill in the missing steps:
1. call to order
2. reading and approval of the minutes
3. reports of standing committees
4. reports of special committees
5.
6. new business
7.
8.
1) call to order   3) reports of standing committees   6) new business

---

B55. Now list *all eight* steps in the order of business.
5) unfinished business   7) announcements   8) adjournment

You are now ready to begin Set C, Making a Motion. The answer to the last frame in Set B is given below.
1) call to order   2) reading and approval of the minutes   3) reports of standing committees 4) reports of special committees   5) unfinished business   6) new business   7) announcements 8) adjournment

MAKING A MOTION

C1. The person who conducts or presides over the meeting is called the *chairman*. During a business meeting the _____ will direct and regulate the activities.

C2. The chairman—or "chair" as he is sometimes called—presides over the business meetings of an _____.
chairman

C3. To be able to participate in a meeting, a member must gain the right to speak. The first step in gaining this right is to *address the chair*. Thus anytime a member wishes to speak in a meeting, he must first _____ the chair.
organization

C4. Addressing the chair is very similar to a student's raising his hand in that both mean that someone's attention is being sought. When a member addresses the chair, he simply wants the chair's _____.
address

C5. The first step in gaining the right to speak in a business meeting is to _____ the chair.
attention

C6. A member addresses the chair by saying, "Mr. Chairman" or "Madam Chairman." When he has said this, the chairman knows that a member wishes to _____.
address

C7. After a member has addressed the chair, he must be *recognized* by the chair before he can speak. Thus the second step in gaining the right to speak is to await _____ from the chair.
speak

C8. The chair recognizes a member by saying, "The Chair recognizes Mr. . . ." If the member has addressed the chair by saying, "_____ _____," the chair will usually recognize him by saying, "_____ _____ _____ Mr. . . ."
recognition

C9. The chair would recognize Mr. John Doe by saying, "The Chair recognizes Mr. Doe." This would give Mr. Doe the right to _____.
Mr. Chairman · The Chair recognizes

C10. If Mr. John H. Smith has addressed the chair, he would know he had been recognized when the chair said, "_____ _____ _____ _____ _____."
speak

C11. Upon being recognized, a member has the *floor* or the right to speak. If you want recognition, you must address the chair. If the chair recognizes you, then you have the _____, or the right to speak.
The Chair recognizes Mr. Smith

C12. Having the floor is the same as having the _____ _____ _____.
floor

C13. The steps in gaining the floor or the right to speak are:
1. address the _____
2. await _____ from the chair
3. rise and speak
right to speak

C14. You should now know how to gain the floor in a business meeting. List (in your own words) the *three* steps used in gaining the floor.
chair · recognition

C15. If a member of an organization wishes to propose any action (ask the group to do something), he must state his proposal as a *motion*. A clear but brief statement of a proposed action is called a _____.
1) address the chair   2) await recognition from the chair   3) rise and speak

C16. If a member wants the organization to do something such as buy furniture, dismiss a member, or give money to charity, he would state this proposed action as a _____.
motion

C17. A motion that proposes some new action is sometimes called an original main _____.
motion

C18. When a person makes an original main motion, he is proposing that the group take some kind of _____ on a new item of business.
motion

C19. All business is brought before an organization by using the motion. Another name for the motion proposing something new is _____ _____ _____.
action

C20. Original main motions will hereafter be referred to as simply main _____; other motions will be referred to by their specific names.
original main motion

C21. Action is proposed in a business meeting by using the _____ _____ _____, which is commonly referred to as simply a _____ _____.
motions

C22. Main motions deal with any subject; therefore, if a member wants the group to donate $10 to the Red Cross, he would propose this action in a _____ _____.
original main motion · main motion

C23. Main motions are recommendations to an organization to take some definite _____.
main motion

C24. A main motion must be stated clearly and simply so that all the members will _____ it.
action

C25. Main motions should be stated _____ and simply so that there is no misunderstanding.
understand

C26. The proper way to state a main motion is to introduce it with the three words "I move that." If a member wishes to make a main motion that the organization buy new furniture, he would simply say, "_____ _____ _____ we buy new furniture."

clearly

C27. How would you make a motion to paint the clubroom red? Write out your motion.

I move that

C28. How would you make a motion to buy pink drapes for the clubroom?

"I move that we paint the clubroom red."

C29. As a member of an organization, you wish to make a motion that the group give $100 to charity. The procedure to follow would be:

1. You must first _____ _____ _____.
2. The chair will then _____ you.
3. At this point you have the floor and will state your main motion. Write out your motion.

"I move that we buy pink drapes for the clubroom."

C30. Which of the following main motions is well worded?

1. "Mr. Chairman, I move that this organization buy $500 worth of Savings Bonds."
2. "Mr. Chairman, I move that we definitely consider giving some money to charity."

1) address the chair   2) recognize   3) "I move that we give $100 to charity."

C31. Again which of the following main motions are well worded?

1. "I move that we give $50 to the Red Cross."
2. "I move that we give some money to the Community Chest."
3. "I move that we write all the people we can think of and invite them to join our club."
4. "I move that we write all persons eligible and invite them to join our club at the next meeting in January."
5. "I move that we give Henry all the money he needs for his New York trip."

1

C32. Since you must gain the floor to make a main motion, your first step is to _____ the chair.
1 · 5

C33. The second step is to await _____ by the chair.
address

C34. After you have been recognized, you may state your _____ _____ .
recognition

C35. After a main motion has been made, a *second* is required to show that one other member approves of having the matter considered, and NOT necessarily that he approves of the motion itself. A person seconds a motion by simply saying, "I _____ the motion."
main motion

C36. The reason for requiring a second to a main motion is to show that someone other than the maker of the motion wishes to consider the _____ .
second

C37. Mr. Smith has made a main motion to paint the clubroom red. If Mr. Jones wishes to consider this motion, he may _____ the motion by saying "_____ _____ _____ _____ ."
motion

C38. There is no need to address the chair and be recognized in order to second a main motion. Immediately after a main motion is made, a member may _____ the motion if he wishes to have it considered.
second · I second the motion

C39. It is not necessary to gain recognition to _____ a main motion.
second.

C40. After the main motion has been seconded, the chair will open the floor for *debate* on the motion. During this period of _____ the members may argue for and against the motion.
second

C41. If Mr. Jones makes a motion that you do NOT approve of, then during the _____ period you may gain the floor and argue against it.
debate

C42. If, instead, you *approve* of a motion that has been made and would like to see it passed, then during the debate period you may argue _____ the motion.
debate

C43. Besides being used for argument for and against the main motion, the debate period can also be used for *amending* the motion. A formal change or modification of a main motion is called an _____. (Amending will be discussed in Set D.)
for

C44. The motion before the group at any one moment is called the *question*. After the debating and amending period is over, the chair will ask the group if they are ready to vote on the _____.
amendment

C45. When the debate and the amending seem to be over, then the chair will ask the group if they are ready to _____ on the _____.
question or motion

C46. If the group is ready to vote, they will join in a general chorus of "Question." Upon receiving this approval, the chair will state the question (or motion) again before the vote is taken. The chair will say, "The _____ is. . . ."
vote · question or motion

C47. After the debate on a main motion has stopped, then the procedure is as follows:
1. The chair will ask if the group is ready _____ _____.
2. The group will answer with "_____."
3. The chair will restate the _____ before the vote is taken.
question or motion

C48. There are two other commonly used ways to close or end debate. A member may move the previous question (which will be covered in Set E), or a member may simply call the question. Debate on a question may be ended by:
1. the chairman stating, "Are you ready to vote?"
2. a member moving the previous question
3. a member _____ the question
1) to vote (or, for the question)   2) Question   3) question or motion

---

C49. We have discussed the way a chairman may put the question to close debate. To move the previous question will be discussed later. Now we will discuss the method of closing debate by calling the _____.
calling

C50. To call the question, a member simply states, "I call the previous question." This means that he wishes to vote now on the _____ before the group.
question

C51. After a call for the previous question, the chair will state that the question has been called. If his statement is followed by a general chorus of "Question" or "Yes" or by silence, then he assumes that the group is ready to _____ on the question.
question or motion

C52. If some of the members wish to continue debate after the question has been called, they may do so if it fails to pass by a two-thirds vote. If it fails, then debate will continue until the question is called again, a member moves the previous question, or the chairman puts the question by asking, "Are you ready to _____?"
vote

C53. There are, of course, two votes that must be taken: the vote for the motion, or the *affirmative* vote, and the vote _____ the motion, or the *negative* vote.
vote

C54. The vote may be taken any way the chair sees fit (show of hands, voice vote, ballot, etc.), but the chair must be sure to call for both sides of the vote. In other words, he must call for both the _____ vote and the negative vote.
against

C55. In taking the vote, the affirmative vote must be called for first. After the affirmative is taken, then the chair will call for the _____ vote.
affirmative

C56. The affirmative vote is taken to discover the number of people _____ the motion, and the negative vote is taken to discover the number _____ the motion.
negative

C57. The _____ vote is always taken first.
for · against

C58. When taking a vote, the chairman should specify the precise method of voting. Thus, when taking a vote, the chairman will say, "All in favor say 'yes,' " or "will stand," and then pause to allow time for the members who are for the motion to _____.
affirmative

C59. After the affirmative vote has been taken, the chairman will say, "All opposed say 'no.' " This will give the members who are _____ the motion an opportunity to vote.
vote

C60. When taking the vote in a meeting, the chair will first call for those in favor of the motion and then call for those _____ to the motion.
against

C61. The two votes called for by the chairman are the affirmative and negative. He calls for the affirmative vote by saying, "_____ _____ _____ say 'yes.' " He calls for the negative vote by saying, "_____ _____ say 'no.' "
opposed

C62. A voice vote should NOT be taken in determining a fraction vote. That is, in trying to determine if two-thirds or three-fourths of the members voting are in favor of the motion, the chairman should have the members either raise their hands or stand rather than have them _____ "yes" or "no."

All in favor · All opposed

C63. The vote required to pass a main motion is a simple majority, which is at least one more than one-half of the members voting. If the final tally in a vote is 6 affirmative and 5 negative, then the motion is passed by a _____ _____.

say

C64. At least one more than one-half of the members voting for one side is what we call a simple _____.

simple majority

C65. If the following votes passed by a simple majority, write "yes;" if they did not, write "no."
1. 10 affirmative, 8 negative
2. 5 affirmative, 4 negative
3. 8 affirmative, 9 negative

majority

C66. The other vote commonly used in business meetings is *two-thirds*. If a motion is passed by two-thirds, it simply means that two-thirds of the members voted *for* the motion. If the final tally in a vote is 15 affirmative and 7 negative, then the vote is passed by _____.

1) yes   2) yes 3) no

C67. A simple method for determining a two-thirds vote is to multiply the negative vote by two. If the product is equal to or less than the affirmative vote, then the motion is passed by _____.

two-thirds

C68. If the negative vote is multiplied by two and the product is larger than the affirmative vote, then the motion fails to pass by _____.

two-thirds

C69. You can easily determine whether a vote passed by two-thirds by multiplying the negative vote by _____.
two-thirds

C70. If, after multiplying by two, the product is equal to or less than the _____ vote, then the motion is passed by _____.
two

C71. There are fifteen members in an organization, and they all vote affirmatively or negatively on a motion. If the motion passes by *two-thirds*, the affirmative vote has to be *at least* _____ votes, and the negative vote *could not be more than* _____ votes.
affirmative · two-thirds

C72. If the following votes would pass by two-thirds, write "yes"; if not, write "no." (Remember, multiply the negative vote by two, and if the product is equal to or less than the affirmative vote, there is a two-thirds passing vote.)
1. 10 affirmative, 8 negative
2. 21 affirmative, 7 negative
3. 14 affirmative, 7 negative
ten · five

C73. After the votes have been counted, the chair will announce the results as passed or failed. If the vote required was a simple majority and the final tally was 27 affirmative and 13 negative, then the chair would announce that the motion _____.
1) no   2) yes   3) yes

C74. The chairman must always take both sides of the vote. This means he must take both the affirmative and _____ votes.
passed

C75. The reason the chair must always take both votes is to give each member a chance to participate and to signify his like or dislike of a motion. Even though the *affirmative* vote gives the passing majority needed, it is the chair's duty to call for the _____ vote.
negative

C76. After the vote has been taken and the results announced, the motion is officially disposed of, and the only way a person can change his vote is by using a special motion which will be studied later. Thus after the chair announces the voting results no one can _____ his vote.
negative

C77. If the affirmative vote is the only vote that has been taken, a member who voted affirmatively may withdraw his vote before the chairman calls for the _____ vote.
change

C78. A member can change his _____ from affirmative to negative, or vice versa, after both votes have been taken and prior to the chairman's announcement of the results.
negative

C79. If both votes have been taken, can a member change his vote? Yes or no?
vote

C80. If the affirmative vote has been taken, a member who voted affirmatively can withdraw his _____ and then vote negatively when the chair asks for the negative vote.
yes

C81. When can a member change his vote? (In your own words.)
vote

C82. At what point is it out of order for a member to change his vote? (In your own words.)
anytime before the results are announced

C83. Complete the following statements.
1. A statement of a proposed action is a _____.
2. Before having the floor, a member must _____ the chair and be _____.
3. Immediately after a motion is made, a _____ is required.
4. If a member wishes to change the motion, he may do so in the debate period by an _____.
after both votes have been taken and the chair has announced the results

You are now ready to begin Set D, Amending a Motion. The answer to the last frame in Set C is given below.

1) motion, main motion, or original main motion
2) address · recognized   3) second
4) amendment

Set D
AMENDING A MOTION

D1. An amendment is a proposal for a change or modification of a motion. You may _____ by *adding* something to the motion, *deleting* or *striking* something from the motion, or *substituting* a word, phrase, sentence, paragraph, or section.

D2. Amendments are used to change or modify a _____.
amend

D3. If a member wishes to change or modify another member's main motion, he can do so by _____ the motion.
motion

D4. To amend a main motion, a member would say, "I move that we amend the motion by . . .," stating the change he wishes to make in the motion. If he wishes to amend a main motion by striking the word "red," he would say, "I move that we _____ the motion by _____ the word 'red.' "
amending

D5. An amendment is a formal _____ or modification of a motion.
amend · striking or deleting

D6. An amendment is treated in the same manner as a main motion. Someone other than the maker of the amendment must wish to consider the change; therefore, an amendment requires a _____.
change

D7. The amendment, like the main motion, must be thrown open for _____ after being seconded.
second

D8. The amendment and the main motion are similar in that both are introduced by the three words "_____ _____ _____," both require a _____, and both are thrown open for _____ by the group.
debate

D9. A formal proposal for action in a business meeting is known as a _____ _____, and a formal proposal for a change or modification of a motion is called an _____.
I move that · second · debate

D10. We may amend by three methods:
1. *deletion:* taking something from the motion
2. *substitution:* replacing a word, phrase, sentence, etc., of the motion
3. _____: attaching something new to the motion
main motion · amendment

D11. Amendments are used to mold the motion into an acceptable form which will express the will of the organization. We may amend by addition, _____, and _____.
addition

D12. List the *three* methods of amending.
substitution · deletion

D13. Amendments are used to mold the motion into a form acceptable to at least a majority of the members of the _____.
1) addition   2) substitution   3) deletion

D14. The following is an example of an amendment by _____: "I move that we leave out (delete) the word 'farm' in 'farm policy.' "
organization or club

D15. The following is an example of an amendment by _____: "I move that we insert the word 'farm' before the word 'policy.' "
deletion

D16. If it is necessary to make numerous changes in a main motion, it may be better to substitute a whole new motion rather than make numerous _____.
addition

D17. To change six or eight different words or items in a single motion, it may be best to amend by _____ a whole new motion for the original motion.
amendments

D18. Great care should be exercised in amending by substituting a whole new motion for the original motion. To _____ the motion of painting the classroom for the motion of buying a new bus would not be a proper use of this type of amending procedure.
substituting

D19. This is an example of an amendment by _____: "I move that we exchange the following motion for the present motion. . . ."
substitute

D20. The three methods of amending are (in any order) by _____, by _____, and by _____.
substitution

D21. The purpose of amending is to change or modify the motion so that it is more acceptable to a _____ of the members of the organization.
substitution · addition · deletion

D22. Any amendment that is made must have a second and must be opened for _____ by the group.
majority

D23. The amendments we have discussed are amendments to the motion itself, or what we call *first degree* amendments. If we wish, however, we may amend a first degree amendment with what we call a *second degree* amendment. There are, therefore, two kinds of amendments: the _____ degree and the _____ degree.
debate

D24. Amendments to the motion are called first degree amendments. Amendments to the first degree amendments are called _____ _____ amendments. There can be no third, fourth, fifth, etc., degree amendments.
first · second

D25. The amendments applied to the _____ are called first degree amendments and may be amended by _____ _____ amendments.
second degree

D26. The amendment in number 1 below is an example of a _____ degree amendment, and number 2 is an example of a _____ degree amendment.
1. "I move that we amend the motion by adding the words 'state farm policy.' "
2. "I move that we amend the amendment by deleting the word 'state.' "
motion · second degree

D27. There can be an amendment to the motion and an amendment to the _____.
first · second

D28. There can be a first degree amendment and a second degree amendment but never a _____ degree amendment.
amendment

D29. The first degree amendment can be amended, but the _____ degree amendment cannot be amended.
third

D30. When the second degree amendment has been disposed of (voted on), then *another* second degree amendment can be made. But remember that the second degree amendment cannot be _____.
second

D31. If it is necessary to make a large number of first and second degree amendments, it may be more advantageous to amend by substituting a whole new *motion* for the intended amended _____.
amended

D32. When a first degree amendment has been disposed of (voted on), then another _____ _____ amendment can be made.
motion

D33. The motion, therefore, is amended by the _____ degree amendment. This amendment may then be amended by a _____ degree amendment. But this is as far as we may go, for there can be no _____ degree amendments.
first degree

D34. There is really nothing complicated about amending a motion if we remember the following:
1. Amending takes place after the motion has been seconded and the floor is open for _____.
2. A motion may be amended by a _____ degree amendment.
3. The first degree amendment may then be amended by a _____ degree amendment.
first · second · third

D35. Amendments must be voted on in *reverse* order. The second degree amendment (if one has been made) must be disposed of first; then the vote can be taken on the _____ _____ amendment.
debate · first · second ·

D36. After taking the vote on the first degree amendment, the vote can then be taken on the original _____.
first degree

D37. If you have made a motion and I have amended it, which will be voted on first — the motion or the amendment?
motion

D38. If you make a motion and I amend it and then John Doe amends my amendment, in what order will the votes be taken?
the amendment

D39. In disposing of a motion and its amendments, the _____ _____ _____ is voted on first, then the _____ _____ _____, and finally the motion itself.
1) John Doe's second degree amendment   2) my first degree amendment   3) your motion

D40. Voting in _____ order is the rule to remember in voting on amendments.
second degree amendment · first degree amendment

D41. An amendment is made, seconded, and thrown open for debate. This debate must be limited to the debate of the _____ and not extend to a debate of the original motion.
reverse

D42. The vote required to pass a motion or amendment is a simple majority. If the vote on a second degree amendment is 8 affirmative and 7 negative, the amendment _____ by a simple majority.
amendment

D43. The vote required to pass a motion is a _____ _____.
passes

D44. The vote required to pass an amendment is a _____ _____.
simple majority

D45. A final important rule to remember about amendments is that all amendments must be _germane;_ that is, an amendment must be on or relate to the subject to be amended. All amendments to a motion must be _____ to the subject of the motion.
simple majority

D46. An amendment must be _germane_ to the subject to be amended. A first degree amendment to a main motion must be _____ to the subject of that main motion.
germane

D47. If all _____ _____ amendments must be germane to the subject of the motion being amended and all second degree amendments must be germane to the subject of the first degree amendments, then all second degree amendments must be germane to the subject of the motion being amended.
germane

33

D48. All first degree amendments must be germane to the subject of the main motion. All _____ degree amendments must be germane to the subject being amended.
first degree

D49. If the motion before the group is whether to buy a new school bus for the school and someone moves to substitute the word "horse" for "school bus," the amendment would be improper because it is not germane or related to the _____ of buying a new school bus for the school.
second

D50. It is possible to make an amendment _____ or relate to the subject being amended even though this amendment may be hostile toward or against the wishes of the supporters of the subject being amended.
subject

D51. Amendments may be _____ toward or against the wishes of the supporters of the subject being amended.
germane

D52. On the basis of what you have learned about amending, complete the following statements:

1. We may amend by: _____, deletion, and _____.

2. A motion is amended by a _____ _____ amendment.

3. The vote required to pass a motion or an amendment is a _____ _____.

4. Amendments must be _____ (related) to the subject being amended.
hostile

You are now ready to begin Set E, Classification of Motions. The answer to the last frame in Set D is given below.

1) addition · substitution   2) first degree
3) simple majority   4) germane

Set E
CLASSIFICATION OF MOTIONS

This set will deal generally with the classification, usage, and precedence of the most commonly used motions. Specific rules regarding the vote required, seconding, amendability, debatability, and renewability in the disposition of individual motions are not programed but will be referred to in the chart in *Robert's Rules of Order Revised,* pages 6 through 10.

E1. For convenience, motions are classified into four divisions: (1) privileged motions, (2) subsidiary motions, (3) incidental motions, and (4) main _____.

E2. Each general classification of motions — privileged, subsidiary, incidental, and main — has a general status or relevance of disposition to each other. Main motions do not take *precedence* over any of the other three classes of motions. A main motion, therefore, would not take _____ over a privileged motion.
motions

E3. The term "precedence" as used in parliamentary practice deals with the order of presentation and disposition of motions. If a motion fulfills all the qualifications of procedure including precedence, then we generally say that the motion is in order. For the moment, let us consider only the correct order of precedence of the four general _____ of motions.
precedence

E4. A privileged motion ranks highest in the order of _____.
classifications, types, or kinds

E5. A privileged motion does not relate to the question pending before a group but is of such great importance to the group that it takes _____ over all other questions.
precedence

E6. Subsidiary motions do apply to main motions. This means that subsidiary motions may modify main motions, or postpone action on them, or refer them to committees to investigate and report, etc. Since subsidiary motions apply to main motions, they supersede main motions in the order of _____.
precedence

E7. A subsidiary motion (assuming it is in order) must be *disposed of* before the main motion to which it applies can be _____ _____.
precedence

E8. Privileged motions take precedence over all other motions. Subsidiary motions must be disposed of before the main motions to which they apply can be disposed of. Therefore, privileged motions take precedence over subsidiary and main _____, and subsidiary motions take _____ over main motions.
disposed of

E9. The fourth general classification of motions is the incidental motions. These motions arise out of another question pending before the group and take precedence over the motion out of which they arise. Thus, an incidental motion arising out of a main motion takes precedence over the _____ motion.
motions · precedence

E10. Incidental motions can arise out of or be a result of almost any main or subsidiary motion. Privileged motions, however, still take _____ over incidental motions.
main

E11. Incidental motions take precedence over all motions to which they are incidental but yield precedence to _____ motions.
precedence

E12. Look at the four classifications of motions this way. The classification that ranks highest in precedence is the *privileged motions*. Next in rank are *two* classifications: *incidental motions*, when they arise out of pending motions, and *subsidiary motions*, when no incidental motions are pending. Finally, when none of the other three kinds of motions is pending, there are the _____ *motions*.
privileged

E13. Now, as a brief review of the four classifications of motions, the privileged motions take precedence over _____, subsidiary, and incidental motions.
main

E14. Main motions do not take _____ over any of the other three classifications of motions.
main

E15. Subsidiary motions take precedence over _____ motions but yield precedence to privileged motions.
precedence

E16. Subsidiary motions are subsidiary to (or in some way can affect) original _____ motions.
main

E17. Incidental motions yield precedence to _____ motions but are incidental to both _____ and _____ motions and must be disposed of as they arise.
main

E18. NOTE: Not all subsidiary motions are subject to incidental motions; that is, not all subsidiary motions can have _____ motions applied to them.
privileged · subsidiary · main

E19. Now, let's investigate the various motions that are classified as privileged motions. Remember, they are privileged because they are of great importance to the group and thus rank highest in the order of _____.
incidental

E20. The privileged motions are, in order of precedence among themselves: (1) fix the time of the next meeting, (2) adjourn, (3) recess, (4) question of privilege, and (5) orders of the day. REMEMBER: these five motions are listed in the _____ of precedence among themselves.
precedence

E21. The motion to fix the time of the next meeting ranks highest in the order of _____ among privileged motions. (See *RROR*, page 7.)
order

E22. To fix the time of the _____ _____ is the only motion that is in order after a motion to adjourn or end the meeting has been made, seconded, and stated by the chair.
precedence

E23. To fix _____ _____ _____ _____ _____ _____ is not an amendment to the motion to adjourn.
next meeting

E24. To _____ _____ _____ _____ _____ _____ _____ is the same as moving the time the group will meet again.
the time of the next meeting

E25. It is important to fix the time of the next meeting if the organization does not meet at a regular *time* or date. An organization that does not have regularly scheduled meetings would have to vote at each meeting on the _____ and date of its next meeting.
fix the time of the next meeting

E26. If we want to hold our next meeting at 7:00 p.m. on April 1, the motion to fix _____ _____ _____ _____ _____ _____ would be, "I move that we fix the time of the next meeting for 7:00 p.m. on April 1."
time

E27. How would you move to fix the time of the next meeting for 1:00 p.m. on October 5 in the auditorium? Write out your motion.
the time of the next meeting

E28. The privileged motion that takes precedence over ALL other motions is the motion to

___ ___ ___ ___ ___ ___ ___.

"I move that we fix the time of the next meeting for 1:00 p. m. on October 5 in the auditorium."

E29. To fix the time of the next meeting is the only motion that can be made after the motion to adjourn is passed. Therefore, to ___ ___

___ ___ ___ ___ ___ takes precedence over all other privileged, subsidiary, and main motions.

fix the time of the next meeting

E30. To fix the time of the next meeting takes ___ over all other privileged motions.

fix the time of the next meeting

E31. The second motion to be considered under privileged motions is the motion to *adjourn*. To ___ means to end a meeting permanently.

precedence

E32. During the course of a meeting, we come to a point when we wish to end the meeting. The motion to adjourn is then used to ___ a meeting.

adjourn

E33. The main purpose of the motion to adjourn is to *end* a meeting; however, it may also be used to ___ discussion on a subject.

end

E34. The motion to adjourn can be made at any time during the meeting. Thus if the members want to go home, one member would simply stand and move, "I move that we ___." (This motion naturally needs a second and a vote. See *RROR*, page 6.)

end or stop

E35. Some clubs do not meet at a regular time or date; therefore, the members would have to fix the time of the next meeting before they ___ or end the meeting.

adjourn

E36. In determining precedence, the motion to adjourn would be ranked second. The first ranking motion is to fix ___ ___ ___ ___ ___ ___.

adjourn

E37. If you will remember, the motion to adjourn was stated as being in order anytime during the meeting. This is because to adjourn takes ___ over all main, subsidiary, incidental, and privileged motions except the privileged motion to fix the time of the next meeting.

the time of the next meeting

E38. Let's try the first two again. To fix the time of the next meeting takes precedence over all other motions; therefore, would to fix the time of the next meeting take precedence over the motion to adjourn? Yes or no?

precedence

E39. The motion to adjourn takes precedence over all other motions except the motion to

___ ___ ___ ___ ___ ___ ___.

yes

E40. Now, decide the following case on the basis of the precedence of motions. In a meeting, one member is discussing a main motion when another member moves to adjourn. Assuming the speaker discussing the main motion was not interrupted, is the motion to adjourn in order? Yes or no?

fix the time of the next meeting

E41. To end a meeting permanently, we would use the motion to ___.

yes

E42. If we do not want to adjourn permanently but would like to take a coke or coffee break, we can *dismiss* temporarily through a motion to recess. To recess means that we are temporarily ___ and will reassemble at a later time. (See *RROR*, page 8.)

adjourn

E43. It should be remembered that the motion to _____ only temporarily dismisses a group.
dismissed or adjourned

E44. To recess means we are temporarily *dismissed* for a certain time and will reconvene. It does NOT mean we are permanently _____ as we would be if we adjourned.
recess

E45. To temporarily end a meeting for a period of time, we would use the motion to _____.
dismissed

E46. When you move to recess, you should state the length of the recess. It can be for a few minutes or several hours, but recess means the group is temporarily _____ and will reassemble.
recess

E47. A temporary disbanding of the meeting can be brought about by using the motion to

_____.

dismissed

E48. If it were hot and you had been in a meeting for a couple of hours and faced the possibility of another two hours in the meeting, you could temporarily end the meeting by moving to _____ for fifteen minutes for a coke.
recess

E49. To make the motion to recess for five minutes, you would say, "I move that we recess _____ _____ _____."
recess

E50. Write out a motion to recess two hours for dinner.
for five minutes

E51. To recess is the third ranking privileged motion in the order of _____. Thus, a motion to recess yields precedence to the motions fix the time of the next meeting and adjourn.
"I move that we recess two hours for dinner."

E52. What do we mean when we say that the motion to adjourn takes precedence over the motion to recess? (In your own words.)
precedence

E53. Which motion takes precedence — fix the time of the next meeting or recess?
If both motions are made, the motion to adjourn is considered first.

E54. The fourth highest ranking motion in the order of precedence is the *question of privilege.* Such a motion would, for example, allow you to open the window if it is too hot. The ____ ____ ____, then, is the fourth highest ranking motion.
fix the time of the next meeting

E55. The question of privilege enables the chairman to dispose of a certain request made by a ____ of the organization.
question of privilege

E56. If the room is too hot, a member may rise and ask the chairman if he may raise a window. This would be a question of ____.
member

E57. If there is no objection by another member, the chairman may grant the motion to raise the window, which would be a ____ ____ privilege.
privilege

E58. In making the motion to raise the window, you would say, "I rise to a question ____ ____."
After the chair asks you to state your question, you would proceed to say it was too hot and ask for the window to be raised.
question of

E59. If a member objects to having the window raised, the chair may ask for a second and have the members vote on whether to grant the question ____ ____ to raise the window. (See *RROR,* page 8.)
of privilege

E60. If the members grant the _____ of privilege, the window is raised; if they do not grant the _____ of _____, the window is not raised.
of privilege

E61. How would you use the question of privilege to change seats because it is too cold where you are sitting? Write out your motion.
question · question · privilege

E62. A question of privilege relates to the group's or the individual's comfort. It may also relate to charges against an individual's character which, if true, might incapacitate him for membership. If someone in your organization called you a traitor, you could use the privileged motion of _____ _____ _____ to defend yourself. (Example: Robert M. LaFollette's famous speech before the U. S. Senate entitled, "Free Speech in Wartime," dated October 1917.)
"I rise to a question of privilege. May I change seats due to the draft of cold air in this part of the room?"

E63. Now, let's review the precedence of privileged motions. If a member moves to recess and after this a member rises for a question of privilege, the chairman would rule the _____ _____ _____ out of order because a motion to recess takes _____ over a question of privilege.
question of privilege

E64. Does the motion to adjourn or a question of privilege take precedence?
question of privilege · precedence

E65. If you wish to end the present meeting and meet again at the next regularly scheduled time, you would use the motion to _____.
adjourn

E66. If you wish to end the meeting but your organization does not have a regularly scheduled time or place to meet, you could adjourn and then move to _____ _____ _____ _____ _____ next meeting.
adjourn

E67. Can you move to fix the time of the next meeting after a motion to adjourn has been made? Yes or no?
fix the time of the

___

E68. Can you move to adjourn during old business and still be in order? Yes or no?
yes

___

E69. Rank the following privileged motions from highest to lowest (1 to 4) in the order of precedence: question of privilege, adjourn, fix the time of the next meeting, recess.
yes

___

E70. Now list the *first four* privileged motions in accordance with their ranking to each other and to all other motions.
1) fix the time of the next meeting   2) adjourn
3) recess   4) question of privilege

___

E71. The fifth and final privileged motion is orders of the day. This motion is the lowest ranking privileged _____.
1) fix the time of the next meeting   2) adjourn
3) recess   4) question of privilege

___

E72. A call for the orders of the day is a demand for the organization to conform to its program or order of *business*. It is made when the organization is varying from the order of _____.
motion

___

E73. If an organization does not have an order of business or the order _____ _____ is not being varied, then this motion could not be made.
business

___

E74. This motion, orders of the day, is rather exceptional in that a single member has the right to demand that the group conform to the order of business. A call for the orders _____ _____ _____ takes precedence over all other motions except adjourn, recess, question of privilege, and _____ _____ _____ _____ _____ _____ _____.
of business

E75. It is the duty of the chairman to announce the business to come before the group. If he does this, there will be very little occasion to ever call for the ____ ____ ____ ____.
of the day · fix the time of the next meeting

E76. If a special time has been assigned to debate a particular question and the chairman fails to notice that it is time to take up the motion or thinks the members are too interested in the pending question to be interrupted, any member has a right to call for the ____ ____ ____ ____.
orders of the day

E77. If the orders of the day are called for and passed, then the group will stop debate on the pending question and proceed with the ____ of business. (See *RROR*, page 8.)
orders of the day

E78. If the call for the orders of the day is not passed, the group will continue with the pending business. A second call for the orders of the day is not allowed until the pending ____ is disposed of. (The privileged motion of orders of the day can be treated in several ways and has various exceptions to its disposition; further information about this motion can be found in *RROR*, page 68-71.)
order

E79. We have now discussed all five of the privileged motions. They are, in their order of precedence:
1. fix the time of the next meeting
2. ____
3. ____
4. question of privilege
5. ____ ____ the day.
business

E80. The second general classification of motions to be considered is the subsidiary motions. These motions alter or in some way affect main ____.
2) adjourn   3) recess   5) orders of

E81. Subsidiary motions can be applied to any main motion; since they supersede or take _____ over the main motion, they must be disposed of before the main motion can be acted upon.
motions

E82. If a main motion is on the floor being debated and someone makes the following motion: "I move that we lay this motion on the table," would this subsidiary motion if carried affect the main motion? Yes or no?
precedence

E83. To move that a main motion be laid on the table does, of course, affect the main motion. The first subsidiary motion, in an order of precedence among themselves, is lay on the _____.
yes

E84. Before we can take a motion from the table (to be discussed later), it must be _____ on the table.
table

E85. When we want to lay aside a motion in order to consider more urgent business, we can move to lay the motion on the _____.
laid

E86. The motion lay on the table can be applied to any _____ motion.
table

E87. To lay a motion on the table, you would say, "I move that we _____ _____ _____ _____ _____ _____."
main

E88. If a member has made a main motion to buy a new book but you think the group should vote on increasing dues first, you could move to lay the main _____ _____ _____ _____.
lay the motion on the table

E89. After the vote on raising dues has been taken, then you or some other member could move to take from the table the motion to buy a new book. The more urgent _____ of raising dues has been disposed of, and now the group is ready to consider buying a new book.
motion on the table

E90. When we lay a motion on the table, it can be taken from the table anytime during new business. In this way the organization can lay *aside* one motion in order to consider a more important or urgent motion and then return to the motion that was laid _____.
business, question, or motion

E91. If we lay a motion on the table during the first part of new business, can we take that particular motion from the table during the latter part of new business at the same meeting? Yes or no?
aside

E92. The length of time a motion is laid _____ _____ _____ makes no difference in the status of the motion.
yes

E93. If at the July meeting we voted to lay on the table the motion to buy a new book for the club, could we leave it there until new business in the August meeting? Yes or no?
on the table

E94. If a motion is laid on the table at a meeting in July, could we take that motion from the table in December? Yes or no?
yes

E95. When you wish to lay a motion aside temporarily, or, in other words, *table the motion,* you would say, "I move to _____ _____ _____. . . ," stating the motion to be laid aside.
yes

E96. If a motion has been taken from the table during new business today, it would be out of order to consider a motion to table _____ _____ again until some material progress had been made on the question.
table the motion

E97. To lay on the table is the highest ranking subsidiary motion, yielding only to the privileged motions, and should be considered immediately upon its being moved. To _____ _____ _____ _____ takes precedence over all motions except _____ motions.
the motion

E98. Since this motion needs only a simple majority to pass (see *RROR*, page 7), there is danger that it may be improperly used to suppress debate on a question. Extreme caution should be taken to ensure that the motion to _____ _____ _____ _____ fulfills its object of laying aside pending business in order to consider more urgent matters.
lay on the table · privileged

E99. If a main motion has been amended or is in the act of being amended (an amendment is under debate) and a motion to lay on the table is passed, then the main motion and all the amendments (passed and proposed) are laid on the _____.
lay on the table

E100. If you want to put aside a motion, you would move to table _____ _____, or lay on the table.
table

E101. Does the motion to lay on the table or the motion to adjourn take precedence?
the motion

E102. If you wish to delay action on a motion only temporarily, you would move to _____ _____ _____.
adjourn

E103. Now, let's move on to the second ranking subsidiary motion, which is to move the previous question. This motion ranks _____ in precedence among subsidiary motions.
table the motion

E104. A call for the previous _____ means that an immediate vote is wanted on the motion being debated.
second

E105. A member can move to vote _____ by saying, "I move the previous question."
question

E106. To make a subsidiary motion to vote immediately on the motion being debated, you would say, "I move the _____ _____."
immediately or now

E107. A call for the previous question, if passed, stops debate on the question and brings it to an immediate _____.
previous question

E108. To stop the debate and amending of a motion, you would say, "I move the _____ _____."
vote

E109. Moving the previous question means you wish to vote _____ on the pending motion.
previous question

E110. If the motion to move the previous _____ fails to pass by a two-thirds vote, then debate will continue on the original motion as if the previous question had never been moved. (See *RROR*, page 81).
immediately or now

E111. A call for the previous question applies only to the question pending before the group unless otherwise qualified. If a main motion has been made and an amendment to this main motion is being debated, a call for the previous _____, if passed, would mean an immediate vote only on the amendment.
question

E112. Anyone moving the previous question would use the form of, "I move (or demand or call for) the ＿＿ ＿＿ on . . . ," specifying the motion or motions on which it is desired to vote immediately.
question

E113. If the member calling for the previous question does not specify the exact motion, then to what motion is it understood to apply? (Answer in your own words.)
previous question

E114. Sometimes a member moves the previous question because he feels that, if the group votes on the pending question immediately, the motion before the group will fail. If the motion to move the previous question is passed, does this mean the group is in favor of the motion on which the previous question is demanded? Yes or no? the motion pending before the group at the time the previous question is called

---

E115. The subsidiary motion to move the previous question yields to all of the privileged motions but takes precedence over all other subsidiary motions except to lay ＿＿ ＿＿ ＿＿.
no

E116. If the previous question is *ordered* on more than one question, then its effect is not exhausted until all the questions are voted on or disposed of in some other way (i.e., lay on the table). In moving the previous question, a member may ＿＿ an immediate vote on several questions.
on the table

E117. There is one limitation of time to the previous question when it is applied to several questions. If the meeting adjourns before all the questions are brought before the group, then the ＿＿ ＿＿ is exhausted. This means that the passage of the previous question is no longer in effect at the next meeting, and any remaining questions are open to debate and amendment.
order or demand

E118. The effect of an unqualified _____ _____ is terminated as soon as the vote on the pending question is taken.
previous question

E119. If the group passes the motion to move the previous question and then further passes the motion to lay the motion on the table, the effect of the previous question remains with the tabled motion if it is taken from the table during the same session. The tabled motion cannot be taken from the table during the same session and be debated, amended, or have any other subsidiary motion applied to it; it must be _____ on immediately.
previous question

E120. If debate has been going on for some time and you now want to stop debate and vote, you would move the _____ _____.
voted

E121. Let's briefly review the precedence of motions again. The privileged motions take precedence over the subsidiary motions. The order of precedence of the privileged motions is:
1. fix the _____ _____ _____ _____ _____
2. _____ (permanently end a meeting)
3. _____ (temporarily dismiss a group)
4. question of _____
5. _____ _____ _____ day
previous question

E122. The first two subsidiary motions in their order of precedence are:
1. lay on the _____
2. previous _____
1) time of the next meeting   2) adjourn
3) recess   4) privilege   5) orders of the

E123. The third subsidiary motion in the order of precedence is the motion to limit (or extend) debate. The third highest ranking subsidiary motion is to _____ (or extend) _____.
1) table   2) question

E124. The motion to limit debate may be used to limit the time for debating the motion. The time available for debate on any motion could be _____ by saying, "I move that we limit debate to five minutes." (Of course, a second and other requirements must be fulfilled. See *RROR*, page 7.)
limit · debate

E125. To extend debate we would simply say, "I move that we _____ debate to five minutes."
limited or shortened

E126. We can restrict or extend the time for debate on a debatable motion by moving to _____ or _____ debate.
extend

E127. This motion to limit or extend debate may also be used to restrict the number of speakers. If you want to limit debate to only five people, you would say, "I move that we _____ _____ to _____ _____." If you wish to extend this limit to ten people, you would say after five people had debated, "I move that we _____ _____ to _____ _____."
limit · extend

E128. How would you move to limit debate to three people with each of them having only five minutes to speak? (In your own words.)
limit debate · five people · extend debate · ten people

E129. Any motion restricting the time a person can speak, the number of speakers, or the length of speeches in words, etc., would be a subsidiary motion to _____ _____.
"I move that we limit debate to three people with each of them having only five minutes to speak."

E130. Even after the adoption of a motion limiting debate, it is in order to make any of the other subsidiary motions on the pending question. If the motion to which limited debate was applied has not been disposed of before the end of the limited time, then at that time the chair should call for an immediate _____.
limit debate

E131. When the time (speaker, length of speeches, etc.) limit has expired, no further amendments or extensions can be made, and an _____ vote is taken.

vote

E132. To place limits on or extend the limits of a question can be accomplished by the motion to _____ or _____ _____. This is the third highest ranking subsidiary motion in the order of _____.

immediate

E133. If you want to restrict the number of people who will be allowed to debate a topic, you would use the subsidiary motion to _____ _____.

limit · extend debate · precedence

E134. The motion to postpone definitely (or to a certain time) is the next highest ranking _____ motion.

limit debate

E135. The motion to postpone _____ is used to delay action on a main motion until a later time and/or date.

subsidiary

E136. To delay action on a main motion until a later date is done by postponing _____ (to a certain _____).

definitely

E137. A specific date or time is always stated in the motion to postpone _____.

definitely · time

E138. You must state the specific date or _____ at which you wish to resume consideration of a motion when you move to _____ _____.

definitely

E139. If you wish to debate a main motion during the last thirty minutes of the meeting, you would move to _____ the debate of the motion until the last thirty minutes. (See *RROR*, page 8).

time · postpone definitely

E140. The meeting is to adjourn at 2:00 p.m. You wish to postpone debate on a main motion until the last ten minutes of the meeting and would therefore move to _____ debate of the motion until 1:50 p.m.
postpone

E141. In moving to resume consideration of a main motion at a later time, you would say, "I move that we _____ the question . . . ," stating the date and/or time for reconsideration.
postpone

E142. To delay action on a motion until a certain time, you would use the motion to _____ _____.
postpone

E143. If you wish to postpone the pending question until after a talk by Dr. Smith, you would simply say, "_____ _____ _____ _____ _____ the question until after Dr. Smith's talk."
postpone definitely

E144. If you wish to postpone the question to the next meeting, the form of the motion would be, "I move that we _____ the question to the _____ _____." The postponed motion would then become a general order for that meeting, taking precedence over new business.
I move that we postpone

E145. When you move to postpone a question _____, giving the next meeting as the time for reconsideration, you are in fact stating that the organization make the postponed question part of the next meeting's business.
postpone · next meeting

E146. By designating a particular time and date to consider a motion, you are making it an "order of the day." If it is not disposed of then, it becomes old _____ at the next meeting.
definitely

E147. If you wish to ensure that a question will not be crowded out by other matters, you would add to the motion to postpone _____ the phrase "and be made a special order."
business

E148. A motion to consider a question during the last thirty minutes of a meeting could be, "I move that the question be postponed and be made a _____ _____ for the last thirty minutes of this meeting."
definitely

E149. To postpone to a certain time does not automatically make the motion a special order. If you wish to make it a _____ order, then you must specify it as such.
special order

E150. If a motion is designated as a special _____, the vote required is two-thirds; to postpone definitely requires only a simple majority. (See *RROR*, page 8.)
special

E151. Before going on to the last three subsidiary motions, let's review the privileged and subsidiary motions already covered. Do the privileged motions take precedence over the subsidiary motions? Yes or no?
order

E152. List the privileged motions in their order of precedence:
1. _____ _____ _____ _____ _____ _____ _____
2. _____
3. _____
4. question _____ _____
5. orders _____ _____ _____
yes

E153. The first four subsidiary motions are:
1. lay _____ _____ _____
2. previous _____
3. _____ (or extend) _____
4. postpone _____
1) fix the time of the next meeting   2) adjourn
3) recess   4) of privilege   5) of the day

E154. Is the motion to adjourn in order at any time after the reading and approval of the minutes? Yes or no?
1) on the table 2) question 3) limit · debate
4) definitely

E155. To end the meeting temporarily for a coffee break, you would use the motion to _____.
yes

E156. If you want to close debate and vote immediately on a *question*, you would move the

_____ _____.

recess

E157. If you want to set aside a pending question in order to consider more urgent matters, you would use the motion to _____ _____

_____ _____.

previous question

E158. If someone calls you a traitor or makes other derogatory remarks about you, you could rise to a _____ _____ _____ in order to defend yourself.
lay on the table

E159. What motion would you use to designate the time the next meeting would be held?
question of privilege

E160. Does the motion to recess or the motion to limit debate take precedence?
fix the time of the next meeting

E161. When a motion is on the floor being debated and another motion is made, one way to determine if the second motion is proper is to consider the _____ of the two motions.
recess

E162. Now we will continue to investigate the rest of the subsidiary motions in their order of _____. The next motion is to refer (or commit) to a committee. (See *RROR*, page 7.)
precedence

E163. One of the reasons for referring a subject to a committee is to have it thoroughly investigated. Thus the motion to refer ____ ____ ____ could be used if the group wants more research done.·
precedence

E164. If we allow a committee to bring in additional information on the subject being debated, this means that the subject was originally ____ to a ____ for investigation.
to a committee

E165. If we pass the motion to ____ ____ ____ ____, this means that the committee should further investigate and study the motion before it is again discussed by the entire group.
referred · committee

E166. The committee or *group* to which a motion is referred is generally smaller than the whole ____.
refer to a committee

E167. Another reason for referring a subject to a committee is to save time during the regular meeting and yet fully discover all the various facts about the subject. A smaller group known as a ____ can investigate the subject and report its findings to the larger group.
group

E168. How many people will be on the committee, when the committee will report, and any other necessary information can be designated by the person making the motion. He could, for example, say, "I move that the motion . . . be referred ____ ____ ____ of three persons to report at the next meeting."
committee

E169. If the person making the motion to refer to a committee does not specify how many persons are to be on the committee or when the report is due, the chairman assumes this duty. Therefore, the number, date, etc., of the committee can be designated by the ____.
to a committee

E170. If the committee members are not designated, the chairman may refer the motion to an already established committee, or he may ask for nominations to serve on a _____ to investigate the subject.
chairman

E171. A good general rule to follow in designating a leader of a committee is to name the leader first and then the rest of the committee. This way, the leader will always be the _____ person named by the chairman.
committee

E172. If a person is interested enough in having further information on a main motion that he moves the motion be referred to a committee, he would be a good one to put on the _____ to help investigate the subject.
first

E173. Generally, the maker of the motion to _____ _____ _____ _____ either has knowledge about the question or an interest in it and thus would be a good member of the committee.
committee

E174. The maker of the motion to _____ _____ _____ _____ may designate the members to be on the committee (subject to approval of the group) in order to guarantee that the committee members are not hostile toward the question to be investigated.
refer to a committee

E175. A hostile committee is one that is _____ the adoption of the subject under discussion.
refer to a committee

E176. Since a _____ committee is against the question, it may therefore cause the question to be lost because of a negative report, no report, etc.
against

E177. On occasion, the entire group or organization may wish to consider a question informally as a *committee*. When the whole group wishes to discuss a question informally, the group moves to a _____ of the whole.
hostile

E178. Committee of the whole means that every member present will be considered a member of the _____.
committee

E179. The motions committee of the whole and refer to a _____ are equal in precedence.
committee

E180. A committee of the whole does not limit the number of members on the _____; instead, all the members of the group are members of the committee.
committee

E181. Unlike the motion to refer to a committee, the motion committee of the whole means that all the members of the group will be members of the committee of the _____ and that the subject will be discussed NOT in the future but immediately. (Exception: the group may wait until other regular business is finished.)
committee

E182. The motion committee of the _____ is used when an organization wishes to discuss the pending question informally.
whole

E183. To move into a _____ _____ _____ whole enables the members to discuss a given motion freely and informally without having to record the discussion officially.
whole

E184. The motion _____ of the _____ was first used in the late sixteenth and early seventeenth centuries to enable members of the House of Commons to attack the Crown without running the risk of losing their heads.
committee of the

E185. Today, in the legislatures of states which require the admission of the press at all regular meetings, the senators may move to a ____ ____ ____ ____ in order to discuss state business without the press being present.
committee · whole

E186. Within an organization where each member can speak only once on a subject (for example, the U. S. Senate), moving to a ____ ____ ____ ____ enables a person to speak as often as he wishes.
committee of the whole

E187. Consensus means that the members agree without *voting*. If a group cannot arrive at a consensus, then the group must ____ in order to arrive at a solution (majority rule).
committee of the whole

E188. The committee of the whole tries to arrive at a consensus, but if it cannot, it must ____ on the solution and try to get a majority to favor one single solution.
vote

E189. The committee of the ____ tries to arrive at a consensus.
vote

E190. The committee of the whole does not make a report as such; rather, the whole group discusses the pending motion in an informal atmosphere. Good group discussion rules should apply during the discussion period, and the group should try to solve the problem by reaching a ____ rather than by voting.
whole

E191. While a group is in a *committee* of the whole, the regular chairman relinquishes his "chair" to a temporary chairman of the ____.
consensus

E192. When a ____ ____ ____ ____ wishes to adjourn, a motion is made that the committee rise and report.
committee

E193. The motion to rise in a _____ _____
_____ _____ is equivalent to the motion to adjourn in a regular business meeting and is in
order at any time.
committee of the whole

E194. We have considered two motions to
refer business to a committee. They are: (1) refer to a _____ and (2) _____ _____ _____ _____.
committee of the whole

E195. These two motions to refer rank the
_____ in the order of precedence.
1) committee   2) committee of the whole

E196. Both of these motions deal with estab-
lishing a _____ to investigate the subject.
same

E197. In order to obtain further information
by having representatives of the group investigate
the main motion, we would use the subsidiary
motion to _____ _____ _____ _____.
committee

E198. The two motions that refer main motions to a committee are:
1. _____ _____ _____ committee
2. committee _____ _____ _____
refer to a committee

E199. The motions to refer yield to all privileged motions and to the following subsidiary
motions:
1. lay on the _____
2. previous _____
3. _____ (or extend) debate
4. _____ _____ _____ certain time
1) refer to a   2) of the whole

E200. If, after a motion to refer _____ _____
_____ has been made, seconded, and stated by
the chairman, another member rises and moves
to proceed into a committee of the _____, would
the motion committee of the whole take precedence? Yes or no? (Remember: both rank equally
in precedence.)
1) table   2) question   3) limit   4) postpone to a

E201. If you wish to have five members investigate a subject and report to the organization at the next meeting, you would rise and say, "I move that we _____ this question to a _____ of five to report at the _____ _____."
to a committee · whole · no

E202. If you wish to discuss the pending question informally and freely, you would stand and say, "I move that we consider the resolution as if in a _____ _____ _____ whole."
refer · committee · next meeting

E203. The next subsidiary motion, to amend a motion, has been discussed previously in Set D. To amend ranks after the motions to refer in the order of _____.
committee of the

E204. Let's briefly review the motion to _____, change or modify, another motion.
precedence

E205. When we _____ another motion, we change it in some way. There are two degrees of amendments: (1) first _____ and (2) _____ _____. (See *RROR*, page 7.)
amend

E206. An amendment must be germane to the *subject* it is amending. This means that the amendment must relate to the same _____ as the motion being amended.
amend · degree · second degree

E207. If this motion is vague in your mind, go back and review Set D to refresh yourself on how to _____ a motion.
subject

E208. If a motion to refer to a committee is on the floor being debated, would a motion to amend the main motion be in order? Yes or no?
amend

E209. The final subsidiary motion to be considered is to postpone indefinitely. This motion takes precedence only over main motions and yields to all privileged, incidental, and other subsidiary _____.
no

E210. If you want to do away with a motion and decrease the chances of it ever coming up again, you would use the motion to _____ indefinitely. (See *RROR*, page 8.)
motions

E211. This motion is made by saying, "I move that we _____ _____ the motion . . . ," stating the motion.
postpone

E212. The real object of this motion is not to postpone action on the motion but to reject the pending motion without voting on it. If we pass the motion to postpone the main question _____, then this main question is postponed for an indefinite period of time.
postpone indefinitely

E213. This subsidiary motion to _____ _____ is often used to give the opponents of a main question an idea as to their numerical strength. It can act for them as a straw vote on the main question.
indefinitely

E214. To postpone indefinitely also provides a means of disposing of a main _____ on which it may be embarrassing for the group to vote yes or no.
postpone indefinitely

E215. To _____ _____ also provides a way of disposing of an ill-advised motion.
motion or question

E216. A main motion that has been postponed _____ may not be renewed at the same meeting.
postpone indefinitely

E217. If we vote and pass to postpone indefinitely, the only way we can reintroduce the postponed motion is to make a completely new _____ during new business no sooner than the next regular business meeting.
indefinitely

E218. If a member moves to buy a pink elephant for the club mascot and will not withdraw his motion, then you could move to _____ _____ and, if passed, reduce the chances of this motion ever coming up again.
motion

E219. To postpone indefinitely does not suppress *debate* on the main question; therefore, it allows more _____ on the subject of the main question.
postpone indefinitely

E220. To postpone indefinitely gives the opponents of the main question an opportunity to kill it without actually voting on the _____ motion.
debate

E221. If the opponents of the main motion fail to pass the motion to postpone indefinitely, then the group has to vote on the _____ motion.
main

E222. If you want to try to do away with a motion and virtually eliminate its chances of ever coming up again, what motion would you use?
main

E223. The subsidiary motion to postpone indefinitely takes precedence over _____ motions.
postpone indefinitely

E224. Does the motion to amend take precedence over the motion to postpone indefinitely? Yes or no?
main

E225. Do privileged motions take precedence over the subsidiary motion to postpone indefi-nitely? Yes or no?

yes

E226. Does the motion to adjourn take prece-dence over the motion to amend? Yes or no?

yes

E227. The subsidiary motions in their order of precedence are:
1. lay on the _____
2. previous _____
3. _____ or _____ debate
4. _____ definitely
5. _____ _____ _____ committee or _____ of the

_____
6. _____ (change or alter a motion)
7. postpone _____

yes

E228. The privileged motions in their order of precedence are:
1. to fix the _____ of the next meeting.
2. _____ (end a meeting)
3. _____ (temporarily take a break)
4. _____ _____ privilege
5. orders _____ _____ _____

1) table 2) question 3) limit · extend 4) post-pone 5) refer to a · committee · whole 6) amend 7) indefinitely

---

E229. If you want to delay action on a motion until 6:30 on July 11, 1961, you would use the motion to _____ _____ _____ _____ _____.

1) time 2) adjourn 3) recess 4) question of 5) of the day

E230. Does postpone to a certain time take precedence over postpone indefinitely? Yes or no?

postpone to a certain time

E231. Would a motion to move the previous question be in order while we are discussing whether to postpone indefinitely? Yes or no?

yes

E232. If you want the group to discuss the main motion informally, you would use the subsidiary motion of moving to a _____ _____ _____ _____.
yes

E233. If you want to have a group of three members investigate a main motion and report back to the group at the next meeting, you would move to _____ _____ _____ _____.
committee of the whole

E234. What are the four general classifications of motions?
1. _____ motions
2. subsidiary _____
3. _____ motions
4. incidental _____
refer to a committee

E235. The next general classification of motions to be considered is main motions. These motions are the lowest in *precedence* of the four classifications of motions and do NOT have any order of _____ among themselves.
1) privileged   2) motions   3) main   4) motions

E236. The first kind of motion to be considered under this heading is the motion that proposes some new action to be taken up by the group and is the *main* vehicle by which business is brought before the group. These motions are called _____ motions (the same name as the general classification of this group of motions).
precedence

E237. Unlike subsidiary and privileged motions, which have an order of precedence, main motions do NOT have an order of _____. Therefore, one main motion does not take precedence over another.
main

E238. If one main motion is on the floor and another main motion is made before the first one is disposed of, the second main motion is out of _____.
precedence

E239. If a main motion is on the floor being debated and a member moves to amend this main motion, the amendment would take _____ over the main motion and have to be disposed of before the main motion. The motion to amend is a _____ motion, and subsidiary motions take *precedence* over main motions. If the amendment is passed, it would affect the main motion in some way.
order

E240. A main motion is a clear but brief statement of a proposed action. The procedure used in making a motion is:
1. address the chair
2. await recognition from the _____ .
3. rise and make the motion
(See Set C for review of how to make a motion.)
precedence · subsidiary

E241. There are five motions that fall under the classification of main motions. Since there is NO order of precedence among main motions, it does not matter in what order they are listed.
1. main _____
2. reconsider
3. rescind
4. make a special order of business
5. take from the table
chair

E242. Is there any order of precedence among these five main motions? Yes or no?
motions

E243. The next motion to be considered under the classification of main motions is the motion to take from the table. The first motion considered under *main* motions was a _____ motion.
no

E244. Only a motion that has been laid on the table can be taken from the _____. (See *RROR*, page 8.)
main

E245. When we take a motion from the table, it means that some time previously the motion was laid ____ ____ ____ or postponed temporarily by the group for more urgent business.
table

E246. A question is supposed to be laid on the table only temporarily, with the expectation of resuming its consideration after the disposal of the interrupting question. The motion to take ____ ____ ____ the previously tabled motion would be in order immediately after disposing of the interrupting question.
on the table

E247. To take a motion from the table means that now we wish to ____ this motion again.
from the table

E248. We can only take from the table motions that were placed on the ____ at an earlier time.
consider or debate

E249. If we placed a motion on the table at our last meeting and now during either new or unfinished business we wish to debate this motion further, we would say, "I move that we ____ ____ ____ ____ the motion . . . ," stating the exact motion.
table

E250. If we want to take a motion from the table at the same meeting or some later meeting, we would move to take the motion ____ ____ ____.
take from the table

E251. If a motion is tabled, the only way this motion can be brought before the group again is by moving, "I move that we ____ ____ ____ ____. . . ."
from the table

E252. Can we move to take a motion from the table during new business? Yes or no?
take from the table

E253. If you want to debate further a motion that has been set aside temporarily by laying it on the table, you would move to _____ _____ _____ _____ this motion.

yes

E254. The next motion to be studied is called reconsider. To reconsider deals with changing the group's decision (vote) on *main motions*. To reconsider guards against hasty action taken on _____ motions.

take from the table

E255. If you voted in *favor* of a motion and it passed but later you want to change your vote on that main motion, you can. You can change it by the motion to reconsider. In order for you to make this motion, however, you must have voted in _____ of the main motion and not against it. (See *RROR*, page 8.)

main

E256. This motion to reconsider an action taken earlier by the group gives the members an opportunity to change their _____ if they change their minds.

favor

E257. In case you voted "yes" and the motion *failed*, then you would be out of order in making the motion to reconsider the vote on the main _____.

vote or decision

E258. On each main motion there is an affirmative (yes) vote and negative (no) vote. If the main motion passes, then we would assume the _____ votes were more than the negative votes.

motion

E259. If the affirmative votes were more than the negative votes and the motion passed, then anyone voting affirmatively (yes) could move to _____ the vote taken.

affirmative or yes

E260. If you voted "yes" on a main motion and the majority of other members voted "no" and the motion lost, then you could not move to _____ the motion because you voted on the losing side.
reconsider

E261. In order for you to move to reconsider, you must have voted on the side that won the decision on the main motion — commonly called the *prevailing* side — and not on the _____ side, which did not win the vote.
reconsider

E262. If the prevailing side (the side that won) was the "no" votes on a main motion, then in order for you to move to _____ the vote taken you must have voted "no" originally.
losing

E263. The prevailing side is the side that wins the decision, and it can be either the _____ or "no" votes.
reconsider

E264. If a group votes 10 in favor and 9 against a main motion and the motion carries, which side is the prevailing side? The "yes" or "no" votes?
"yes"

E265. If a group votes 10 in favor and 9 against a main motion and the motion passes, would you be in order in moving to reconsider if you voted against the motion? Yes or no?
"yes" votes

E266. If you were one of the members who voted against a main motion and the motion failed, would you be in order in moving to _____ the voting and change your vote from against to in favor? Yes or no?
no

E267. If a motion to reconsider is made, this should indicate that at least one person who voted on the prevailing side has changed his mind and wishes to change his _____.
reconsider · yes

E268. The motion to reconsider relates only to the vote taken and not to the relevant motion itself. If the motion to _____ carries, debate is reopened as if no vote had been taken on the relevant matter.
vote

E269. When we reconsider a vote, we are dealing only with the _____ taken and not with the motion on which we voted.
reconsider

E270. The first rule to remember about the motion to reconsider is that the maker must have voted on the _____ side. A second rule is that this motion must be made at the same meeting or on the day following the original vote.
vote

E271. The motion to reconsider must be taken either at the same meeting or on the following day for it to be in _____. Otherwise, this motion would be out of order, and it would not matter whether the members had changed their minds or not.
prevailing or winning

E272. To make the motion to reconsider, you would simply say, "I move to _____ the action taken by this group on . . . ," stating the main motion.
order

E273. The chairman may and should ask a person moving to reconsider a main motion, "Did you vote on the _____ side?" If he did, he would answer "yes," and the motion would be in order.
reconsider

E274. If the chairman asks you, "Did you vote on the prevailing side?" and you answer "no," then the chairman would rule you out of order, and the motion to _____ would be disregarded.
prevailing

E275. This motion to _____, or to change the vote on a motion, is very complicated. It cannot be applied to certain motions, and, if adopted, it has various effects. (For further discussion of this motion, see *RROR*, pages 156-168.)
reconsider

E276. The motion to reconsider relates to the _____ taken on a motion. The next motion to be studied relates to the motion rather than to the vote. This motion is called rescind.
reconsider

E277. To rescind means to cancel a motion. If an organization wishes to void a motion previously passed, it can do so by the motion to _____. (See *RROR*, page 8.)
vote

E278. You would be in order in moving to rescind a vote taken at a previous meeting without having voted on the _____ side (the side that won).
rescind

E279. To rescind is not in order at the same meeting that the original vote was taken. If you wish to move to _____ action on a main motion, you must make this motion at a following meeting.
prevailing

E280. If the group voted today to buy a pink elephant as a club mascot and you want to rescind this motion, you must wait until the _____ meeting to make this motion.
rescind

E281. If the motion to _____ is passed, it nullifies the motion itself; therefore, the motion is defeated, and debate is NOT reopened.
following or next

E282. The motion to rescind should not be made just to change the vote on a motion if the motion to reconsider, which deals with the _____, can be properly used.
rescind

E283. To rescind means to cancel or nullify the whole motion. This motion is not in order at the same meeting at which the original vote was taken, but it is in order at any meeting _____ the meeting at which the vote was taken.
vote

E284. If the motion to rescind passes, the relevant motion is canceled; but if the motion fails, the relevant motion is not _____.
following or after

E285. If you wish to move to rescind a motion passed at a previous meeting, you would say, "I move to _____ the action taken on . . . (stating the motion) at . . . (giving the meeting)."
canceled

E286. Now for a quick review. To _____ means to cancel a motion. To reconsider the action taken by the group means at least one person who voted on the prevailing side wishes to change his _____ on the motion.
rescind

E287. You can move to *cancel* the action of the group on a main motion without having voted on the prevailing side by moving to _____ the main motion previously passed by the group.
rescind · vote

E288. If you voted on the prevailing side (the side that won the decision) but you want to *cancel* the action taken by the group rather than just change the vote, what motion would you make? Rescind or reconsider?
rescind

E289. If the club passes a motion to buy a new flag and you voted against this motion, would you be out of order in moving to reconsider? Yes or no? Why (in your own words)?
rescind

E290. At this *same* meeting and under the same circumstances, would you be out of order in moving to rescind the action taken to buy the new flag? Yes or no? Why (in your own words)?
yes · you must have voted on the prevailing side in order to move to reconsider

---

E291. The motions to change decisions are:
1. _____ (if you voted on the prevailing side)
2. _____ (cancel a motion passed at a previous meeting)
yes · you cannot move to rescind at the same meeting that the motion was made and voted on

---

E292. We have previously discussed the call for the orders of the day and postpone definitely (to a certain time). These two motions correspond closely to the next motion included under the classification of main _____, the motion to make a special order of business.
reconsider · rescind

E293. Remember that the motion to postpone definitely does not automatically become a special order unless it is explicitly stated that it be made a _____ order.
motions

E294. The orders of the day may be called in order to discuss a motion that was postponed definitely or made a special order of _____.
special

E295. To make a _____ _____ of business temporarily changes the regular order of business.
business

E296. We can use the motion special order of business to set a *special* time to consider a _____ question.
special order.

E297. To make a special order of business means that the group wishes to consider a question out of the regular order of _____ but still within the rules of parliamentary procedure and the organization.
special

E298. If your club meets at 7:00 p.m. and you want to consider the problem of lack of members at 7:30, then you would say, "I move that we make 'lack of members' a special ____ ____ ____ at 7:30."
business

E299. If the club votes to discuss lack of members at 7:30, then at that hour the president will announce that "lack of members" will be discussed — even if the club is discussing another subject at the time — because the club had previously passed the motion to make a ____ ____ ____ ____ of this subject at 7:30.
order of business

E300. To make a special order of business ensures the discussion of a subject at a ____ time or place during the regular order of business.
special order of business

E301. We studied earlier the eight steps in the order of business. The motion ____ ____ of business allows an organization to deviate from this regular order of business in order to discuss a subject at a specific time or place.
special, specific, given, etc.

E302. We have now covered three of the four general classifications of motions. The three general classifications already studied are: (1) privileged motions, (2) subsidiary motions, and (3) ____ motions. The fourth classification is *incidental motions.*
special order

E303. *Incidental* motions are motions that are ____ to a question pending before the group and should be decided before any other business is taken up.
main

E304. Incidental motions arise out of another question that is pending and therefore take ____ over the motion to which they are incidental and must be decided first.
incidental

E305. Privileged motions take precedence over all other classes of motions; therefore, privileged motions take precedence over incidental _____.
precedence

E306. In order for an incidental motion to take precedence over a certain motion, it has to be legitimately incidental to that motion. Thus, incidental _____ can take precedence over subsidiary motions.
motions

E307. There is NO order of _____ among the incidental motions.
motions

E308. The first _____ motion to be discussed is point of order. (See *RROR*, page 7 under "Appeal.")
precedence

E309. To make a point of order means to bring some error of procedure to the attention of the chair and other members so that it can be corrected. This ensures proper order of _____ during the meetings.
incidental

E310. To make a point of order, you rise and state, "I rise to a point of _____." The chairman replies, "State your point," and you do.
procedure or business

E311. If discussion on a main motion is out of order, a member may rise and make the motion, "I rise to a _____ _____ _____."
order

E312. If the chairman does not call for the votes in favor of a motion but only for those opposed to the motion, a member may _____ _____ _____ _____ _____ _____ and remind the chairman of his failure to call for the affirmative votes.
point of order

E313. If a member stands and starts to talk without being recognized by the chair, you may ____ ____ ____ ____ ____ ____ and note the correct procedure.
rise to a point of order

E314. Generally, a point of order is made by saying, "I ____ to a ____ ____ ____."
rise to a point of order

E315. If the chairman thinks your point of order is well taken, the procedure is corrected. If he does not think it is ____ ____, the order of business proceeds without correction.
rise · point of order

E316. If the chairman says, "Five voted to adjourn, six voted not to adjourn and a simple majority is needed, therefore we are adjourned," you could rise to a ____ ____ ____ and note the incorrect procedure of the chairman.
well taken

E317. To correct a breach in the order of procedure or a wrong decision by the chairman, you would make a ____ ____ ____.
point of order

E318. If the chairman does not think your point is ____ ____, the group may overrule the chairman's decision by using another motion — appeal from the decision of the chair.
point of order

E319 If your point ____ ____ is not accepted by the chairman but it is the correct procedure, you may appeal from the decision of the chair, which is the next incidental motion. (See *RROR*, page 7 under "Appeal.")
well taken

E320. To appeal from the decision of the chair means to override a decision made by the chairman. It is like the U.S. Senate overriding the President's veto of a bill. You would make the appeal by saying, "I ____ from the decision of the chair."
of order

E321. It must be remembered that the power of the chairman is limited only by the power given him by the _____ of an organization.
appeal

E322. If the members disapprove of the chairman's decision on a motion, they may appeal from _____ _____ _____ _____ _____ .
members

E323. To make the motion to appeal from the decision of the chair, you would say, "I _____ _____ _____ _____ _____ _____ _____ ." If this motion is seconded, the chair should state clearly the question at issue.
the decision of the chair

E324. After your motion to appeal from the _____ _____ _____ _____ has been seconded, the chairman will say, "The chair's decision has been appealed from."
appeal from the decision of the chair

E325. If an appeal is made, the chair will say, "The chair's decision has been _____ from; all those in favor of sustaining the chair's decision raise your hands" . . . "all those opposed raise your hands."
decision of the chair

E326. Suppose there are 5 votes for and 4 votes against a motion that needs a two-thirds vote to pass and the chair says, "The motion carries (passes)." If you rise to a point of order and the chair rules you out of order, what motion could you now make to keep the chairman from making the wrong decision? (Write out the motion.)
appealed

E327. The chair's decision is the same as a vote by the chairman. When you appeal _____ _____ _____ _____ _____ , you are saying, "I think we should all have an equal 'vote' on this matter."
I appeal from the decision of the chair.

E328. Only a simple majority is needed to sustain a decision of the chair. If there is a tie vote by the members, the chair's decision is sustained because his decision is also classified as a vote, which gives the ＿＿＿ majority necessary to sustain the decision.

from the decision of the chair

E329. If a chairman makes a decision you do not like, you would appeal from ＿＿＿ ＿＿＿ ＿＿＿ ＿＿＿ ＿＿＿. This motion is in order every time the chairman makes a decision.

simple

E330. An appeal from the decision of the chair is another motion that must be decided on as it is raised, and it is in order every time the ＿＿＿ makes a decision for the group without letting the group vote on the matter.

the decision of the chair

E331. The next incidental motion is to suspend the rules. The first two incidental motions were:
1. point ＿＿＿ ＿＿＿
2. appeal ＿＿＿ ＿＿＿ ＿＿＿ ＿＿＿ ＿＿＿ ＿＿＿

chair or chairman

E332. To suspend the *rules* is used to temporarily set aside the regular procedure or ＿＿＿ governing the organization. We can NOT suspend the constitution and by-laws, only the standing rules of an organization. (See *RROR*, page 8.)

1) of order   2) from the decision of the chair

E333. In order to dispose of a special bit of business which is against the rules of an organization, we would move to ＿＿＿ the rules.

rules

E334. If you have a very important item of business that you want brought before the group at some time earlier than the designated time, you would move to ＿＿＿ ＿＿＿ ＿＿＿.

suspend

E335. To suspend _____ _____ is different from making a special order of business in that suspending the rules allows you to take up some business that is against the standing rules of the organization.
suspend the rules

E336. The main motion to make a special order of business is generally used to designate a future time and date when a question will be discussed. The motion to _____ the rules is used· in order to do something that the standing rules of the organization would normally not allow.
the rules

E337. Thus to suspend the rules and to make a special order of business differ in that to suspend _____ _____ refers to temporarily setting aside the rules of an organization that would make it impossible to consider a particular question.
suspend

E338. You could move to suspend the rules in order to bring up a special item of business which otherwise would be out of _____.
the rules

E339. When you move to suspend the _____, it could mean that you have something important to discuss that cannot wait unitl later.
order

E340. When you move to _____ _____ _____, you must specify the object for the suspension, and only that object will be considered if the motion passes.
rules

E341. The fourth incidental _____ to be considered is the motion which allows a member to object to consideration of a question moved by another member.
suspend the rules

E342. If you do not think a motion that has been made is worth _consideration_ by the group, you can object to _____.
motion

E343. In order to express your objection to discussing a particular motion, you would say, "I object _____ _____ of this motion."
consideration

E344. You would object to consideration if you think the motion made is irrelevant, objectionable, or unworthy of the members' time and thus you do not want it _____.
to consideration

E345. If a motion is not in the best interest of the group, you could use the incidental motion _____ _____ _____ of the motion.
considered, debated, or discussed

E346. If a person makes a motion that is unimportant or is not related to the business of the meeting, you could _____ _____ _____.
object to consideration

E347. To object to consideration has special qualifications in that it must be made right after the second and before debate begins on a motion. Therefore, to _____ _____ _____ affects the status and debate of a motion.
object to consideration

E348. You must object to consideration of a motion prior to any debate on it or you will be out of _____.
object to consideration

E349. The motion object _____ _____ must be made right after the main motion is seconded and before debate begins.
order

E350. When is the motion object to consideration in order?
1. after the second and before debate
2. before the second
3. after debate has been started
to consideration

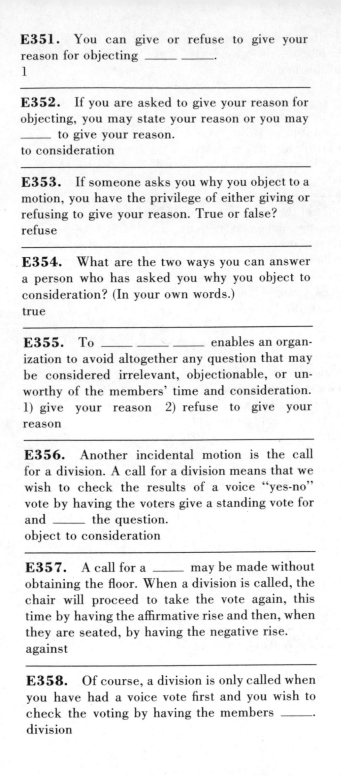

E351. You can give or refuse to give your reason for objecting _____ _____.
1

E352. If you are asked to give your reason for objecting, you may state your reason or you may _____ to give your reason.
to consideration

E353. If someone asks you why you object to a motion, you have the privilege of either giving or refusing to give your reason. True or false?
refuse

E354. What are the two ways you can answer a person who has asked you why you object to consideration? (In your own words.)
true

E355. To _____ _____ _____ enables an organization to avoid altogether any question that may be considered irrelevant, objectionable, or unworthy of the members' time and consideration.
1) give your reason 2) refuse to give your reason

E356. Another incidental motion is the call for a division. A call for a division means that we wish to check the results of a voice "yes-no" vote by having the voters give a standing vote for and _____ the question.
object to consideration

E357. A call for a _____ may be made without obtaining the floor. When a division is called, the chair will proceed to take the vote again, this time by having the affirmative rise and then, when they are seated, by having the negative rise.
against

E358. Of course, a division is only called when you have had a voice vote first and you wish to check the voting by having the members _____.
division

E359. The call _____ _____ _____ is made by simply saying, "I call for a division," or "I doubt the vote," or "Division."
stand

E360. An extreme version of this call for a _____ would be to actually divide the members of the assembly as if choosing up sides. All those in favor of the motion would rise and go to one side of the room; all those against would rise and go to the other side. Remember, this is the extreme way.
for a division

E361. There may be times during a meeting when members wish to obtain information concerning the rules of parliamentary procedure, ask questions of the speaker, or make some other pertinent _request_. Two motions that enable members to _____ such information are parliamentary inquiry and request for information.
division

E362. The first motion, _parliamentary_ inquiry, enables a member who is not quite clear on _____ law to gain enlightenment on a point.
request or obtain

E363. By requesting a parliamentary inquiry, a member is able to find out the correct procedure during a meeting. Therefore, a parliamentary inquiry takes _____ over all motions except privileged motions if it is correctly made. (See _RROR_, page 8.)
parliamentary

E364. If you do not know the correct procedure to follow, you may ask the chairman for a _____ inquiry in order to find out.
precedence

E365. Every member of an organization should have a good knowledge of parliamentary procedure, but if a point is in doubt, it is best to consult the chairman or a reference book by requesting a parliamentary _____.
parliamentary

E366. The parliamentary inquiry enables any member to seek advice about the correct _____ procedure to follow.
inquiry

E367. The incidental motion that allows a member to find out the correct parliamentary procedure to follow is the _____ _____.
parliamentary

E368. To request a parliamentary inquiry, you would say, "I rise to a _____ _____"; the chairman would then ask you to state your inquiry.
parliamentary inquiry

E369. Any point of order may be preceded or followed by a _____ inquiry if the correct procedure is in doubt.
parliamentary inquiry

E370. If a parliamentary _____ interrupts a speaker and there is no reason to answer it until the speaker has closed his remarks, then the answer may wait until the speaker is finished.
parliamentary

E371. The second motion that enables a member to make a *request* is the motion _____ for information.
inquiry

E372. A _____ _____ _____ relating to the pending business is treated just as a parliamentary _____. (See *RROR*, page 8 under "Parliamentary Inquiry.")
request

E373. The motion request for information enables a member to find out additional information about a subject. Therefore, _____ _____ _____ takes precedence over all motions except privileged motions if it is correctly made.
request for information · inquiry

E374. The motion request for information is very useful in that it enables a member to request additional _____ about a subject being discussed.
request for information

E375. A request for information is similar to a parliamentary _____; a request for information allows a member to ask questions concerning any pending business, whereas a parliamentary inquiry allows a member to ask questions about the procedure to be used.
information

E376. The request for information is directed to the chairman. If the chairman can answer the request, he should do so; however, if the _____ cannot answer the question, he may direct the question to a member of the organization to be answered.
inquiry

E377. If one member has the floor and is talking and another member wants to ask the speaker a question concerning his speech, he could ask, "Will the speaker yield to a question?" This is the same as using the motion request _____

_____.
chairman

E378. If the speaker on the floor will yield to a question, then the member making the request for _____ will ask the question; if not, the member making the _____ _____ _____ will have to sit down and the speaker will continue.
for information

E379. In case the speaker on the floor does yield to the question, the question should be directed to the *chairman,* and the answer should be directed to the _____ also. This procedure does not allow one member of the organization to argue directly with another.
information · request for information

E380. The final incidental motion to be studied is the motion to withdraw a motion. The originator of a motion may move to withdraw his _____ any time before the voting on the question has commenced. (See *RROR,* page 8.)
chairman

E381. The motion to withdraw a motion is in order at any time during the debate on a main motion and can be moved only by the person who made the main _____ being debated.
motion

E382. It should be emphasized that this motion, withdraw a motion, is in order any time during the debate on a main motion, but only the _____ of the main motion can move to withdraw the motion.
motion

E383. If you make a motion, you may move to withdraw your motion during the debate on it by saying, "I move to _____ my motion ... ," stating the motion.
maker or originator

E384. Only the maker of the motion can make the incidental motion to withdraw the _____.
withdraw

E385. The maker of a motion may request to withdraw his _____ if he changes his mind after it has been made, seconded, and opened for debate.
motion

E386. If you make a motion and while it is being debated you change your mind and wish to withdraw it, you would say, "I move to _____ _____ motion ... ," stating the motion.
motion

E387. We studied earlier that once a motion was made, seconded, and restated by the chairman, that motion became the property of the whole _____ or all the members of the organization.
withdraw the

E388. The maker of a motion is the only person who can request to withdraw his motion; but once the group begins debating the motion, the group must give its consent before the motion is _____.
organization, group, club, etc.

E389. If someone objects to the maker withdrawing his motion, then the members must cast their _____ to see if the group will consent to letting the motion be withdrawn.
withdrawn

E390. The person who seconded the motion does not have to agree with the maker of the motion in order for the maker to _____ his motion.
votes

E391. Can the person who seconded the maker's motion request to withdraw the motion? Yes or no?
withdraw

E392. If a person objects to your withdrawing your motion, the group must _____ to give you permission to withdraw it.
no

E393. If there is a fault in the procedure during the debate on a motion to postpone definitely, would it be in order to rise to a point of order? Yes or no?
vote

E394. If an irrelevant and objectionable motion is made, what incidental motion would you use after the second and before debate to stop action on the motion?
yes

E395. If a motion you made is now being debated and you change your mind and wish to cancel the motion, what motion would you use to stop any further discussion?
object to consideration

E396. If you want to ask a question of a member discussing an issue, you would say, "I rise to request _____. Will the speaker yield to a question?"
withdraw the motion

E397. If you are in doubt about a point of parliamentary procedure, you could say, "I rise for a _____ inquiry."
information

E398. If the chairman makes a decision the group does not like, you would appeal _____ _____ _____ of the chair in order to override his decision.
parliamentary

E399. If someone makes a motion that is out of line with the business of the group, you could move to _____ _____ consideration of the question.
from the decision

E400. If a motion you made is now being debated and you change your mind and want to cancel the motion, you would move to _____ _____ _____.
object to

E401. Can you move the previous question while a point of order is being discussed? Yes or no?
withdraw the motion

E402. If you are in doubt about what the procedure should be, would you be in order to rise for a parliamentary inquiry when a motion to adjourn is on the floor? Yes or no?
no

E403. Can the maker of a main motion move to withdraw his motion when this main motion has been amended and the group is debating the *amendment?* Yes or no?
no

E404. If there is an error in procedure, you would say, "I rise to a _____ _____ _____."
no

You are now ready to begin Set F, Officers and Election. The answer to the last frame in Set E is given below.
point of order

88

Set F
OFFICERS AND ELECTIONS

F1. So far we have referred to the leader of an organization as the chairman. He is also called the president. The president, therefore, is the _____ of an organization.

F2. The president is the senior officer and presides over all meetings held by the _____.
chairman

F3. Although we have referred to him as the chairman, the senior officer of an organization is also known as the _____.
organization or members

F4. It is the president's responsibility to serve the members of the _____.
president

F5. It is also the president's responsibility to create the atmosphere for good discussion. To do this he must encourage the members to participate in the activities of the _____.
organization

F6. To encourage participation by the members, the president must arouse the members' interest in the _____ being discussed.
organization

F7. The president should know and understand the members of the organization in order to encourage their _____ in the discussion.
subject, motion, or topic

F8. The president is actually responsible for seeing that *worthwhile* discussion takes place at each meeting. Discussion on any subject connected with the proper business of the meeting is considered _____.
participation or interest

F9. Discussion may arise about any subject the
_____ of an organization consider worthwhile.
worthwhile

F10. If worthwhile business takes place in a
meeting and the meeting progresses rapidly and
effectively, then the _____ is doing his job well.
members

F11. The president can favor no one but must
preside impersonally and impartially. This
means that he must give the same attention and
fairness to each _____ of the organization.
president or chairman

F12. In presiding impersonally, the president
will never state his opinion on the _____ being
discussed.
member

F13. The president acts as an umpire or
referee for the group. This means that he only
keeps order and does not state his _____ on the
subject being discussed.
subject, motion, or question

F14. If for some reason the president is required or wishes to speak on a subject, he must let
someone else (the vice-president) preside. Then
he speaks just as any other _____ would.
opinion

F15. To be able to speak in a meeting, what
must the president do? (In your own words.)
member

F16. The chairman is also impersonal in referring to himself as "the chair" and not as "I."
He refers to the members by name, but he calls
himself "_____ _____."
He must let someone else preside for him before
he may speak.

F17. There are many things the chairman must
be, but the most important is that he must be
interested in the welfare of the _____ that has
elected him its president.
the chair

F18. The senior officer of an organization is called the _____.

organization

F19. The person responsible for encouraging discussion and keeping order in meetings is called the _____.

president or chairman

F20. The president has many duties. One duty is to announce the steps in the order of _____ as they come due.

president or chairman

F21. It might be a good idea for the president to prepare an outline of the eight steps in the order of business to guide him as he presides over the _____.

business

F22. When it is time for the first step in the order of business, the president will say, "The meeting will please come to _____."

meeting

F23. After the meeting has been called to order, the president will say, "The secretary will read the _____ of the last _____."

order

F24. After the reading and approval of the minutes, the president will ask, "Are there any reports from the _____ committees?"

minutes · meeting

F25. After the standing committee reports have been given, the president will ask, "Are there reports from the _____ _____?"

standing

F26. After the special committee reports have been given, but before taking up new business, the president will call for _____ business.

special committees

F27. After the unfinished business has been taken care of, the president will call for _____ business.
unfinished or old

F28. The next step is for the president to ask if there are any _____. This is the time to announce committee meetings, special thanks to someone, etc.
new

F29. The final step is for the president to ask if there is a motion that the meeting _____.
announcements

F30. Another duty of the president is to give the floor to members who address the chair. When a member addresses the chair, the chair will give him the _____ by recognizing him.
adjourn

F31. Each time a member wishes to speak he must address the chair. He must then be _____ by the president before he may speak.
floor

F32. In order to be fair during debate on a motion, the chairman should first _____ the proposer of the motion being debated.
recognized

F33. After the proposer of the motion has had his turn to speak, the chairman should attempt to recognize members from alternate sides of the question being debated. That is, he should try to give the floor to a person speaking against the question, then a person speaking _____ the proposal, and then against, then for, etc., until debate ends.
recognize

F34. In recognizing members, the chairman should give precedence to a *member* who has not spoken on the motion over a _____ who has already spoken.
for

F35. By recognizing only one member at a time, the president will prevent confusion and give each member a chance to _____ without interruption.
member

F36. After a motion has been made, the president should restate the motion to be sure it is understood before it is debated and _____ on.
speak or talk

F37. The president (chairman) sees that all motions and questions arising in a *meeting* are properly presented and debated. In short, he sees that the business in each _____ is carried on efficiently.
voted

F38. The president also decides all questions of parliamentary _____.
meeting

F39. The president must have a good knowledge of parliamentary procedure in order to decide questions arising among the _____.
procedure or inquiry

F40. The president might wish to refer to a good parliamentary procedure *manual* for answers to difficult questions. He should never hesitate to use the _____ if he is in doubt.
members

F41. Probably the most useful manual for reference is *Robert's Rules of Order Revised.* It is a complete manual and will no doubt answer many of the more difficult _____.
manual

F42. *Robert's Rules of Order Revised,* is a very complete _____ of parliamentary procedure.
questions

F43. If the president needs a good reference manual to answer difficult parliamentary procedure questions, he should consult _____ _____ _____ _____ _____.
manual

F44. Although the president may wish to use a manual for the more difficult questions, he cannot be constantly referring to a book for his parliamentary _____.
Robert's Rules of Order Revised

F45. The president can vote on any question, but he should use discretion because of the status of his position. Usually the president votes only to make or break a tie or when the _____ is by secret ballot.
procedure

F46. The president can vote to make or break a _____.
vote

F47. The president of an organization can vote on any _____, but generally he votes only to _____ or _____ a tie vote of the members or when there is a secret ballot.
tie

F48. The president is not _____ to vote but may do so if he wishes.
question or motion · make · break

F49. If there is a tie on a motion requiring a simple majority and the president elects *not* to vote, then the motion remains a tie and therefore _____ to pass.
required

F50. If the votes taken on a motion are 10 affirmative and 10 negative, the president can pass the motion by voting on the _____ side.
fails

F51. If the votes taken on a motion are 21 affirmative and 20 negative, the president can defeat the motion by voting on the _____ side, thus making the vote a _____.
affirmative

F52. If the votes taken are 21 affirmative and 20 negative and the president does not wish to vote, then the motion is _____.
negative · tie

F53. As we have seen, the president may vote in a meeting to _____ or _____ a tie. He is never _____ to vote but may do so if he wishes.
passed

F54. The president is the leader of the organization, but this does not mean that he controls the business of the organization. He is not elected to persuade the members to follow his *ideas* but, instead, to direct the members in carrying out their own _____.
make · break · required

F55. The president is not elected to carry out his own *wishes and desires* but, rather, to carry out the _____ _____ _____ of the members.
ideas

F56. Another officer in an organization is the vice-president. His chief duty is to be prepared to take charge in the absence of the _____.
wishes and desires

F57. When the vice-president acts in the place of the president, he has all the powers of that office. In the president's absence the vice-president will have the same duties that are designated for the _____.
president

F58. If the president wishes to speak on a particular subject during a meeting, the _____ will take over the chair.
president

F59. In addition to being prepared to replace or relieve the president, the _____ will usually serve as head of one of the important committees.
vice-president

F60. One of the duties of the vice-president would be to head one of the important _____ in the organization.
vice-president

F61. A third officer in an organization is the secretary. He acts as an assistant to the president and records the activities of each meeting in the form of minutes. In the absence of the president and vice-president, the _____ will preside.
committees

F62. The secretary keeps a written record of the meetings in the form of _____.
secretary

F63. After being approved, the minutes become a permanent record of the organization's activities. They are kept on file as an objective account of exactly what happened at the _____.
minutes

F64. The first items recorded in the minutes are the name of the organization and the date, time, and place where the _____ was held.
meeting

F65. After this essential information has been given, the minutes will be written in paragraph form and will include every motion that is made, with the name of the person making the _____.
meeting

F66. Every motion that is made will be recorded in the minutes along with the name of the person making the motion. This must be done accurately because these minutes will become a permanent _____ of the organization's activities.
motion

F67. The secretary — and sometimes the president — will sign his name at the end of the _____.
record

F68. The minutes of a meeting will always include every motion that is made along with the _____ of the person making it.
minutes

F69. The minutes will also include the time, date, and _____ of the meeting.
name

F70. What items does the secretary record in the minutes? List them.

place

F71. The secretary is responsible for all the records of the organization and must be able to produce them when requested by the officers or

_____.

name of the organization · time, date, place of the meeting · all motions · names of the makers of the motions

---

F72. There are certain records that the secretary must have at each meeting. One is a roll of all members and all committees. The president may wish to ask for a roll call of the members, or he may want to see the names of the members on a certain _____.

members

F73. The secretary needs to have a roll of all members and a record of all _____ members with him at each meeting.

committee

F74. The secretary should also have a copy of the organization's constitution and by-laws with him at the meetings. The president may ask the secretary to read an article from the organization's _____ _____ _____.

committee

F75. The third item that the secretary should have available at each meeting is a manual of parliamentary procedure. As we mentioned before, one of the best manuals on parliamentary procedure is _____ _____ _____ _____ _____.

constitution and by-laws

F76. This manual should be available for use by the members if they have a question about the _____ _____ being used.

Robert's Rules of Order Revised

F77. We have learned that the secretary should have at least *three* records or documents available at each meeting. List them.
parliamentary procedure

F78. The vice-president and secretary are members of the organization and may make motions, debate, and vote just as any other member. The only officer who cannot make motions and debate in his official position is the _____.
1) manual of parliamentary procedure 2) constitution and by-laws 3) roll of members and committees

---

F79. We have learned that the senior officer and chairman of an organization is the _____.
president

F80. The officer who takes the chair when the president is absent is the _____.
president

F81. Another officer, the _____, is the keeper of the organization's records.
vice-president

F82. The detailed procedure for the election of officers will be found in the organization's constitution and by-laws. The procedure, therefore, will vary from organization to _____.
secretary

F83. Although a few fundamental procedures concerning elections hold true in most organizations, the detailed procedure will be outlined in the organization's _____ _____ _____.
organization

F84. A few weeks before the time to elect new officers, the president will appoint a *nominating* committee. This committee is given the responsibility of _____ a person for each office in the organization.
constitution and by-laws

F85. The _____ committee will bring a list of suggested officers' names to the election meeting.
nominating or naming

F86. The president will call for a report from the nominating committee during new business. When called upon, the chairman of the _____ _____ will give the committee's report.
nominating

F87. The nominating committee will give its report during _____ _____.
nominating committee

F88. After the reading of the nominating committee's report, the president will ask if anyone present wishes to make a further nomination. Any member present may then stand and _____ a person for an office.
new business

F89. Many times a small club will not have a nominating committee, and all of the nominations will have to come from the _____ present at the meeting.
nominate

F90. Whether the nominating takes place through a committee or through nominations from the floor, it should be done during _____ _____.
members

F91. If a member wishes to make a nomination for president from the floor, he would simply say, "I _____ John Doe for president."
new business

F92. A second is not needed when a nomination has been made. The president accepts each name nominated and will allow the members to vote on each of the _____.
nominate

F93. If you wish to nominate Jane Smith for secretary, you would say, "_____ _____ _____ _____ _____ _____."
names, persons, etc.

F94. After you have made your nomination, there would be no need for anyone to _____ the nomination.
I nominate Jane Smith for secretary.

F95. When the president decides that all of the nominations have been made, he will declare the nominations closed. After this no one can make a _____.
second

F96. If a member of the group would like to close the nominations, he may do so by saying, "I move that the _____ be closed." This motion requires a second and vote. (See *RROR*, page 7.)
nomination

F97. There are two ways to close the nominations. One is for the president to _____ _____ _____ _____.
nominations

F98. The second way to close the nominations is for a member of the group to move that the _____ _____ _____.
declare the nominations closed or close the nominations himself

---

F99. The voting in elections may be done any way the organization sees fit. Each person can be voted on after he has been _____, or the members may wish to wait until all the names have been _____ before voting.
nominations be closed

F100. When the voting is by *ballot*, the president must wait until all the nominations have been made so that the _____ can contain all the names.
nominated · nominated

F101. In a ballot election—that is, when the *candidates* are voted on by using a written ballot—the voters are NOT restricted to the _____ on the ballot but may write in other names.
ballot

F102. Candidates may not be written in on the ballot if the organization's constitution and by-laws forbid this practice. If there is no such restriction, then any member may _____ _____ a name or names for office.
candidates or names

F103. Write-in candidates can only be counted when an organization votes by ballot and the _____ and by-laws do not restrict such practice.
write in

F104. A simple majority vote is required to elect the officers unless the organization's _____ and by-laws state otherwise.
constitution

F105. The vote required to elect officers is usually a _____ _____. In some cases the _____ _____ _____ will state that another vote is required.
constitution

F106. If the constitution and by-laws state that a special procedure (or vote) will be followed in the elections, then that procedure must be followed. The *procedures* set forth in the constitution and by-laws take priority over all other _____.

simple majority · constitution and by-laws

You are now ready to begin Set G, Constitution and By-laws. The answer to the last frame in Set F is given below.
procedures

CONSTITUTION AND BY-LAWS

G1. In forming an organization, there are recommended procedures to follow which will allow those people who are interested to _____ a group.

G2. First, discuss with others the idea of forming a club or organization, for a particular purpose and see if a majority would want to _____ such a group.
form or organize

G3. If you find that a majority would be interested in joining, then agree on a time and _____ to hold the first meeting.
form or join

G4. When the time arrives (it is customary to delay beginning the initial meeting fifteen or twenty minutes to be sure everyone interested has arrived), have the person most interested call the meeting to _____.
place

G5. The first item to dispose of is the election of a temporary *chairman* (president). This person, when elected, is called the _____ pro tempore.
order

G6. The chairman *pro tempore*, when elected, will assume the duties of the chair and proceed to the election of a secretary _____ _____.
chairman or president

G7. The secretary pro tempore will, after elected, assume the duties of the _____.
pro tempore

G8. The next item is to discuss the purpose of organizing the group and, after this has been agreed on, to make a motion (or resolution) to

_____.
secretary

G9. The final item to dispose of at the first meeting is to either appoint or elect a group to draw up a proposed _____ and by-laws for the group which will be presented at the next meeting.
organize

G10. The group drawing up the constitution and by-laws would NOT be a *committee* because "_____" is a technical term that is not used until the constitution is approved and the club is official.
constitution

G11. When this is finished, the chairman pro tempore will entertain a motion to _____ and thus end the meeting.
committee

G12. At the end of the first meeting, a time and place for the second meeting could be set by using the motion to fix _____ _____ _____ _____ _____ _____.
adjourn

G13. Sufficient time should be allowed between the first and second meetings so that the group drawing up the _____ _____ _____ can carry out their duty.
the time of the next meeting

G14. At the second meeting, the chairman pro tempore and the secretary _____ _____ will again assume their assigned duties.
constitution and by-laws

G15. The chairman pro tempore will call the meeting to order; the secretary pro tempore will read the minutes of the last meeting and have the members _____ the minutes (as corrected).
pro tempore

G16. The chairman pro tempore will then call for a report from the group drawing up the _____ and by-laws.
approve

G17. Once the constitution and by-laws has been adopted by the members, the election of permanent _____ will follow.
constitution

G18. Once the permanent officers have been elected, the permanent president (chairman) will take over immediately, but the permanent _____ will not take over until the next meeting, since changing secretaries in the middle of the meeting could confuse the recording of the minutes.
officers

G19. After the permanent president (chairman) has taken over, the group will continue in the regular order of _____.
secretary

G20. The group appointed or nominated to draw up a _____ and by-laws can follow a recommended outline of articles.
business

G21. These articles are the ones normally included in the constitution and by-laws when they are combined into a single document. Other documents could take precedence over an individual organization's _____ and by-laws — for example, articles of incorporation, state and federal constitutions, etc.
constitution

G22. A constitution and by-laws could be drawn up by a group before the _____ is formed.
constitution

G23. To make sure everything essential is covered in the _____ and _____ that is drawn up, the group must follow some kind of outline.
organization or club

G24. This outline is composed of articles, each of which is an important point to be covered in the _____ and _____.
constitution · by-laws

G25. A constitution and by-laws is composed of an _____ which contains points called _____.
constitution · by-laws

G26. There are seven of these points or _____ in a constitution and by-laws.
outline · articles

G27. How many articles are usually found in a constitution and by-laws?
articles

G28. The first article included is the *name*. The organization's name is simply stated as a matter of record to designate that this constitution refers to the organization carrying this _____.
seven

G29. The second article is *purposes*. This article presents a general statement of the objectives of the organization and how these _____ are to be attained.
name

G30. After the name and the purposes, the third article is *membership*. This article includes such items as the qualifications of members, the method of selection, the classes of members, and the amount of dues to be paid by _____.
purposes or objectives

G31. What are the first three articles included in a constitution and by-laws? List them.
members

G32. The fourth article is *officers*. This article designates the names and duties of each _____ in the organization.
1) name   2) purposes   3) membership

G33. Article one of the constitution and by-laws is name; article two is _____; article three is membership; article four is _____.
officer

G34. The fifth article is *committees*. This article lists the standing committees and their duties as well as the procedure for forming special _____.
purposes · officers

G35. The sixth article, called *meetings*, includes the frequency of meetings and the procedure for calling special _____.
committees

G36. The definition of a quorum is included under meetings, article number _____.
meetings

G37. A quorum is the minimum number of club members necessary to transact business. The quorum is designated under article number _____ of the _____ _____ _____.
six

G38. The seventh and last article usually found in the constitution and by-laws is called *amendment*. This article states the vote required to _____ the constitution and by-laws.
six · constitution and by-laws

G39. Article seven should also specify the method by which the constitution can be amended, such as prior notice to all members of the intention to _____ the constitution.
amend

G40. This prior notice of amending the constitution can have several forms — circulation of the amendment, written notice of the proposed amendment, or simply a notice that an _____ will be proposed to the constitution.
amend

G41. Fill in the missing articles:
1.
2.
3. membership
4. officers
5. committees
6. meetings
7.
amendment

G42. Again fill in the missing articles:
1. name
2. purposes
3.
4.
5. committees
6.
7. amendment
1) name   2) purposes   7) amendment

G43. Now list all *seven* articles usually included in a constitution and by-laws.
3) membership   4) officers   6) meetings

G44. The organization's constitution and by-laws becomes the basic document of the organization and the supreme authority governing the members of the _____.
1) name 2) purposes 3) membership 4) officers 5) committees 6) meetings 7) amendment

---

G45. The basic document called the _____ and _____ is the supreme authority for an organization.
organization

G46. The basic document called the constitution and by-laws is the supreme _____ for an organization.
constitution · by-laws

G47. Although the constitution and by-laws is the _____ authority, the organization needs a code or manual of parliamentary procedure to regulate its regular business meetings.
authority

G48. The most popular manual is probably *Robert's Rules of Order Revised.* This book is used as a reference and as a supplement to the supreme authority which is the _____ _____ _____.
supreme

G49. The most commonly used reference manual for parliamentary procedure is ____ ____ ____ ____.

constitution and by-laws

G50. Although *Robert's Rules of Order Revised* is used as a reference manual, the supreme and final ____ for procedure and rules is the constitution and by-laws.
Robert's Rules of Order Revised

G51. From what you have learned, complete the following statements:
1. The constitution and by-laws is the supreme ____ for an organization.
2. The most commonly used reference manual for parliamentary procedure is ____ ____ ____ ____ ____.

authority

You have now completed the final set in this program. The answer to the last frame in Set G is given below.
1) authority or document 2) *Robert's Rules of Order Revised*

POST-TEST ON PARLIAMENTARY PROCEDURE

1. Where does the term "parliamentary procedure" come from?

2. List the steps in the order of business.

3. What is the procedure for gaining the floor in a meeting?

4. List the three ways in which a motion may be amended.

5. What is an amendment to the main motion called? What is an amendment to the amendment called?

6. What is a simple majority vote?

7. What is the simplest way to determine a two-thirds majority?

8. Number the following motions in their order of precedence.
_____Amend
_____Lay on the table
_____Adjourn
_____Previous question
_____Recess
_____Main motion proposing some new action
_____Limit debate
_____Question of privilege
_____Fix the time of the next meeting
_____Committee of the whole

9. What motion would you use to:
  a. Find out the proper procedure to make a motion.

  b. Defend yourself against a personal attack.

c. Correct an error in procedure.

d. Override a ruling by the chair.

e. Gain information concerning pending business.

f. Nullify a motion passed at a previous meeting.

g. Dispose of another member's motion without voting on it after debate has begun.

h. Test the voting strength without actually voting on the relevant question.

i. Check the results of a voice vote.

j. Change your vote from "yes" to "no" on a motion just passed.

10. Write *P* for privileged motions, *S* for subsidiary motions, *M* for main motions, and *I* for incidental motions.

_____Previous question
_____Orders of the day
_____Limit debate
_____Object to consideration
_____Postpone indefinitely
_____Lay on the table
_____Take from the table
_____Suspend the rules
_____Postpone definitely
_____Withdraw a motion
_____Refer to a committee
_____Special order of business

11. What special qualifications must be met by a person moving to reconsider?

12. Name the two types of committees and explain how they differ.

13. Mark *T* for true and *F* for false.

_____Parliamentary procedure must be exactly the same for all organizations.

_____It is possible to change or rephrase another member's motion without amending it.

_____The chairman can take an active part in the meeting and voice his views at any time.

_____A motion that is laid on the table will automatically be brought up and voted on at the next meeting.

_____If the chairman is not sure what ruling to make, the safest thing for him to do is to call for a vote.

14. When can the chairman vote?

15. What book is the best reference manual on parliamentary procedure?

16. What is the final and supreme authority governing an organization?

17. List the articles commonly found in a combined constitution and by-laws.

SUGGESTED STUDY OUTLINES

OBJECTIVES

1. An understanding of the basic essentials of parliamentary procedure.
2. An awareness of the theory and practice of good parliamentary procedure.
3. A knowledge of the correct procedures to use in meetings.
4. Poise in administering the various offices of an organization.
5. Better participation as a member in an organization.

CLASS STUDY OUTLINE

1. Have the students take the Pre-test on Parliamentary Procedure, page vi.
2. Explain the general procedure to follow in using *Parliamentary Procedure: A Programed Introduction.* (See the Instructions, page 1.)
3. Designate a time for the completion of the program, but let the students proceed through the program at their own rate. (Average time is seven hours.)
4. Have the students take the Post-test on Parliamentary Procedure, page 109.
5. Organize laboratory club meetings.
   a. Draw up constitution. (See Sample Constitution for Class Use, page 114.)
   b. Assign students to the various offices and committees outlined in the Sample Constitution.
   c. Introduce *Robert's Rules of Order Revised* as parliamentary authority and explain how it should be used.
6. Practice parliamentary procedure in laboratory club meetings. Change officers and have the committees report as outlined in the Roster of Officers, page 116.
7. Hold critique sessions.
   a. Discuss the strategy used by various students in the meetings and review special problems encountered. Emphasize how various motions can be used to increase or decrease the efficiency of an organization.
   b. Assign students to create certain problem situations at the laboratory meeting and then at the following critique session discuss the procedure used.

8. Maintain a permanent record of the minutes and committee reports. Check the minutes periodically to see whether their form and content are correct.
9. Assign students to give critiques of the business meetings of various campus organizations.

INDIVIDUAL STUDY OUTLINE

1. Take the Pre-test on Parliamentary Procedure, page vi.
2. Complete the entire program, *Parliamentary Procedure: A Programed Introduction.* Be sure to read the Instructions on page 1 carefully before you start the program.
3. Keep a record of your answers so that you can review particular problems later in *Robert's Rules of Order Revised.*
4. Use *Robert's Rules of Order Revised* to familiarize yourself with all phases of parliamentary procedure.
    a. Read this book in the order suggested in the Suggestions for the Study of Parliamentary Law on page 305.
    b. Become familiar with the Table of Rules Relating to Motions on pages 6 through 10.
5. Accept every opportunity to participate in business meetings either as a member or as an officer.

SAMPLE CONSTITUTION FOR CLASS USE

CONSTITUTION OF _____

I. *Name of the Organization*
The name of the organization shall be _____.

II. *The Purpose of the Organization*
   A. General statement of objectives
   B. Means of attaining objectives

III. *Membership*
All students in _____ (name of course)
shall be members of this club.

IV. *Officers*
   A. The officers shall be as follows:
      1. Chairman
      2. Parliamentarian
      3. Secretary
   B. The officers shall be appointed by the Roster of Officers (page 116).
   C. The officers' duties:
      1. The chairman shall:
         a. Call the meeting to order on time and proceed with the usual order of business if a quorum is present.
         b. Maintain order in the meeting at all times—one motion and one speaker at a time.
         c. Decide all parliamentary questions with the advice of the parliamentarian.
         d. Preside impartially and impersonally—even referring to himself as "the chair."
         e. State each motion after it has been seconded and before opening debate. After debate, restate the motion before taking the vote. Announce the results after each vote has been taken.
         f. If he wishes to speak, let the parliamentarian take over the chair.
      2. The parliamentarian shall:
         a. Act as an advisor to the chairman on all questions of parliamentary procedure.
         b. Be constantly alert for errors in procedure.
         c. Give a report at the end of each meeting.

3. The secretary shall:
   a. Keep a roll of all members.
   b. Keep a record of all committee members.
   c. Keep minutes of all meetings.
   d. Have a copy of the constitution and by-laws with him at all meetings.
   e. Assist the chairman when called upon.

V. *Committees*
   A. Standing committees:
      1. The standing committees and their duties shall be:
         a. Committee on Discussion—Reports on classroom discussion and suggests topics for discussion and initiates the discussion.
         b. Committee on Progress and Procedure—Reports on students' progress in learning parliamentary procedure and offers suggestions for improvement. Is also responsible for seeing that every motion is used by the end of the course.
         c. Committee on School Problems—Reports on school problems and promotes discussion on these problems.
         d. Committee on Community Improvement—Reports on the problems of the community in which the school is located and promotes discussion on these problems.
         e. Committee on Entertainment—Reports on entertainment worth being seen by the students and promotes discussion on this subject.
      2. The committees will report on the days designated in the Roster of Officers (page 116).
   B. Special committees shall be appointed by the chairman or by a motion from the floor.

VI. *Meetings*
   A. The meetings shall be held _____ (days and hour).
   B. Special meetings shall be called by the instructor.
   C. A quorum shall be _____.
   D. The parliamentary authority shall be *Robert's Rules of Order Revised*.

VII. *Amendments*
   A. Voting on proposed amendments to the constitution must take place on the first regular meeting after the amendment has been proposed. Discussion is in order at both meetings.
   B. The vote required to change the constitution is set at _____.

ROSTER OF OFFICERS

This roster is designed for twenty members and ten meetings.

List the members in alphabetical order:

1. _____ 11. _____

2. _____ 12. _____

3. _____ 13. _____

4. _____ 14. _____

5. _____ 15. _____

6. _____ 16. _____

7. _____ 17. _____

8. _____ 18. _____

9. _____ 19. _____

10. _____ 20. _____

The officers at each meeting will be:

Meeting	Chairman	Parliamentarian	Secretary
I	1	2	4
II	9	5	7
III	3	19	12
IV	11	8	16
V	20	4	17
VI	12	18	13
VII	14	7	2
VIII	10	13	18
IX	17	15	19
X	16	6	1

In case of the absence of any officer, the member who last held that office will fill in. The secretary is responsible for passing on the minutes (in final form) to the new secretary.

List the committee members:

Discussion

1. _____   3. _____

2. _____   4. _____

Progress and Procedure

1. _____   3. _____

2. _____   4. _____

School Problems

1. _____   3. _____

2. _____   4. _____

Community Improvement

1. _____   3. _____

2. _____   4. _____

Entertainment

1. _____   3. _____

2. _____   4. _____

The committees will report as follows:

Committee	*Meeting*
Discussion	1, 3, 6
Progress and Procedure	5, 7, 10
School Problems	4, 7, 9
Community Improvement	2, 8, 10
Entertainment	3, 6, 9

4990